How to Prepare a Sermon

How to Prepare a Sermon

BY

H. E. KNOTT

M. A. (Harvard), B. D., Professor of Homiletics, Eugene
Bible University, Eugene, Oregon

THE STANDARD PUBLISHING COMPANY
CINCINNATI, OHIO

Printed in U. S. A.

PREFACE

THE present work has had its origin in what the author regards as a real need. While a number of books have been published within recent years on preaching, they are, for the most part, in the nature of a general discussion of the subject. Many who are seeking help in the actual work of sermon preparation are without assistance except as they resort to technical works on homiletics.

The purpose of this book is to give a brief, helpful approach to the science of sermon construction on correct homiletical principles.

The questions given at the end of each chapter are intended to suggest discussion for study groups and training-classes. It is hoped that in this field it will meet a long-felt want.

CONTENTS

Contents

Contents

Contents

Contents

INTRODUCTION

NOTHING can ever take the place of preaching in the life and growth of the church. It will ever be true that God is to save the world through "the foolishness of preaching." The admonition of the greatest preacher of his day to his son in the gospel must be followed now if the commission of the Lord is to be executed, "Preach the Word."

It is a notable thing that in this age, when so many people are at sea as regards the things of revelation, there is no great preacher who does not have people to hear him. The churches of those who know how to bring the Word of life to the heart and conscience with power are filled to the doors.

We have long needed a brief, clear statement of the fundamentals in sermon-making. There are certain great principles which must ever be foundational in real preaching; they can not be ignored without a loss of power. Numbers of fine works on homiletics adorn our shelves, but, in the main, they deal with the art of preaching and those things which the average man should know are all too frequently dealt with in but a summary manner. If one has the time and inclination, he will find in "The Theory of Preaching," by Dr. Phelps, a masterful discussion of the "how" of sermon building. But the ordinary man will not wade through the hundreds of pages of this encyclopedic effort in order to gather the kernels which he needs.

Professor Knott, in this work, has given what has long been wanted. Here, in easily accessible form, are the basic principles of correct sermon preparation. Elders and deacons, so-called lay preachers, and earnest personal workers, in addition to colleges, will find that this volume meets their need. Professor Knott's rich experience in the College of the Bible, Glen Iris, Melbourne, Austral., and the years spent at Eugene, Ore., in teaching young men how best to arrange their messages to win men to Christ, and to edify those who have previously named His name, have qualified him to speak this authoritative word on an ever fresh and interesting theme.

JESSE R. KELLEMS.

CHAPTER I.

THE SERMON: ITS DEFINITION AND PURPOSE

OUR word "sermon" comes from the Latin *sermo*, which means "discourse." In its modern significance the word applies to that formal address which is a part of the church service. Vinet has expressed it in his definition as "a discourse incorporated with public worship, designed . . . to conduct to Christian truth those who have not believed it, and to explain and apply it to those who admit it."

The art of preparing and delivering sermons has been made into a branch of theological study known as homiletics. This aspect of ministerial training has been formally stated "as the science that teaches the fundamental principles of public discourse as applied to the proclamation and teaching of divine truth in regular assemblies gathered for the purpose of Christian worship." So, then, the sermon refers to the formal address given in connection with religious services, while the seminary course that is intended to train men in the art of preparing and delivering sermons is designated the study of homiletics.

Probably the most comprehensive and concise definition of a sermon yet published is that given by Phelps in his work on "The Theory of Preaching," where he devotes two chapters to a definition and its discussion. He defines it as "an oral address, to the popular mind, upon religious truth, as contained in the Scriptures, elaborately treated, with a view to persuasion.''

According to this definition, a sermon is a discourse which is ''to the popular mind,'' thus differentiating it from a lecture, which may be technical in character rather than popular, and placing it in a different category from a discussion of some phase of religious thought that can only be apprehended by a few people. How many fail just here by substituting a lecture for a sermon without being conscious that the pulpit is not fulfilling its function.

It is also to be upon ''religious truth.'' Discourses upon civic ideals, biographical essays, and kindred themes may be very interesting, and also very helpful in the same way as a good concert is uplifting, but these are not in the strict sense of the term sermons. They do not give worshipers the specific thing they rightly expect from the pulpit.

Furthermore, it is to be religious truth ''as contained in the Scriptures.'' There are many interesting approaches to religion from the philosophical standpoint, and a keen, analytical mind may enjoy many delights in this realm, but a discussion on these lines is in the field of speculation, and is not upon ''truth contained in the Scriptures.'' The failure to recognize the difference between Biblical truth and human opinions has been one of the most disruptive evils of church history. The first great cleavage in the Christian church grew out of a philosophical speculation. The same tendency to define that which can not be defined, or make a test of fellowship of that which is not clearly revealed, has led to most

of the divisions in modern Protestantism. In the
fundamental things of the gospel it is interesting to
notice the method of Jesus, as may be illustrated in
dealing with the problem of sin. The origin of sin or
evil is always an attractive theme, yet Jesus never
discussed any theory in connection with it. Whenever
He spoke of sin He always recognized it as a fact, and
spoke of a remedy for it. We will certainly come
nearest the method of Jesus, and best fulfill the function of the pulpit, when we keep to facts, "truth
contained in the Scriptures."

This truth is to be "elaborately treated." A
brief talk at a young people's meeting or a prayer-
meeting may be upon religious truth contained in the
Scriptures, but, because of the brief time occupied, may
not be a sermon. To dignify it with that title there
must be an extended treatment of the theme. The
phrase, "elaborately treated," is, of course, a relative
expression. To fulfill this requirement would, at one
time, have involved an hour or an hour and a half,
while to-day the same statement could be made to
apply to twenty minutes or half an hour, the pre-
vailing opinion and practice being on the side of
mercy even here. Some time ago a number of preachers met in an American city and discussed the matter
of the time that ought to be occupied in preaching a
sermon. They came to the conclusion that the best
results could be achieved by preaching for about
twenty-three minutes. Most preachers know that
preparation tendeth to brevity anyhow. There is also
a psychological problem involved here. Many people
in the average congregation are unaccustomed to extended periods of concentration of thought, and if the

sermon is interesting, the strain produces fatigue. This condition is reached with many people after about twenty minutes. Where the speaker is a stranger, or an unusual personality, this condition might not obtain, but for the minister who is not a genius, preaching to the same people every Sunday, discretion, as well as mercy, ought to be a characteristic of his work.

The last part of Phelps' definition introduces us to the purpose of the sermon. It is to be "with a view to persuasion." From the standpoint of the purpose of the discourse, Vinet is even more definite and specific. He says that it is "to conduct to Christian truth those who have not believed it, and to explain and apply it to those who admit it." This coincides exactly with the purpose of preaching as taught by Jesus in His commission to the disciples in which He says: "Go ye therefore, and *make disciples* of all the nations, baptizing them into the name of the Father and of the Son and of the Holy Spirit: *teaching them* to observe all things whatsoever I have commanded you: and lo, I am with you always, even unto the end of the world."[1] Recognizing these two groups of persons—those who are disciples and those who are not—who make up the modern congregation, many preachers have come to use the morning service as a time for addressing themselves to Christians, and the evening service for more definitely leading people to accept the truths of Christianity and ally themselves with Christ's followers. This plan has great value both for the preacher and for his congregation. It keeps his aim in preaching clear,

[1] Matt. 28: 19, 20.

and enables him to address himself to a definite constituency each time. Without some method such as this, the appeal for people to attend two services on Sunday is considerably weakened, and the evening service is naturally deserted. If, however, the congregation understands that the evening service is for a different purpose from that of the morning, and is specially to lead others to a decision for Christ, they can be urged to work for that end and can be expected to attend in order to show their co-operation. The Scriptural objective in preaching is admirably suited to our two Sunday services, and is the best method, no matter whether considered as a matter of policy or the obedience to a divine command.

One thing further, perhaps, ought to be said in defining a sermon. It is not a general discussion of religion, either in the nature of a rambling talk or a running skit on the Scriptures. To be worthy of the name, it must be limited by a clear, definite proposition, and thus be a unit of thought. This, however, will receive more consideration later.

The work of preaching is one of the highest exercises of the soul. To stand before an audience, all the people very much alike, having their struggles and disappointments, hopes and fears, and all those mingled feelings that are common to our modern life—to face such a congregation, and give them the only message that can lift them out of the transient and the sordid into the eternal and sublime; to tell people in terms of our own experience, the unspeakable joy of communion with the Infinite—is a privilege any one might well covet. A preacher recently made the statement that he would not exchange positions with the President of the United States. He was having a wonderful ministry, and this sentiment can be repeated in the life of any man who recognizes the world's great need, and who has a deep conviction of divine truth, having experienced the saving grace of the gospel in his own soul.

Questions on Chapter I.

1. What is the connection between a sermon and homiletics?

2. How would you differentiate at a religious convention between a discourse that is a sermon and one that is not?

3. Should the Biblical purpose in preaching as indicated in Matt. 28: 19, 20 be maintained in the modern pulpit?

4. Would you regard such subjects as higher criticism and evolution as suitable subjects for discussion in the pulpit? Justify your answer.

CHAPTER II.

THE SERMON OUTLINE

THE plan of a sermon is not fundamentally different in its arrangement from other forms of public
discourse. A sermon, indeed, preached without a text
is not any different in form or method of development from an address upon a secular theme. It only
differs from other kinds of discourse in so far as it
takes into consideration a text, which at the beginning may require explanation, or which may become
the basis of divisions, as we shall notice later. The
principles involved apart from these facts, however,
are precisely the same for all kinds of addresses.
This plan of a sermon, or, as it is usually designated,
outline, is a synopsis, a brief, or an epitome of what it
is desired to say, expressed in such form and language
as makes it easy to recall one's ideas. All clear
thinking should be reducible to an outline, no matter
what may be the nature of the theme. When such
grouping is not possible it may be regarded as a fairly
certain indication that one has not thought his way
through his subject. The best outline for each individual is that which is set out in such form and is expressed in such language as to suggest most readily
the thought he desires to develop.

Some preachers have developed a spirit almost approaching contempt for formal outlines. A number of

reasons have contributed, perhaps, to bring about this attitude. Some have thought that it was limiting the work of the Holy Spirit, a careful preparation of what one intends to say not leaving the Divine Spirit free to express Himself. There can be no doubt about this theory being built upon a false foundation. To seek divine help in preparing the message is to depend upon the Spirit's guidance just as much as to wait till one is about to enter the pulpit and then call upon God. The world's greatest preachers have ever been among those whose outlines reveal the most careful preparation.

Another reason for this attitude toward outlines is the fact that some men, who are otherwise capable and may be regarded as fairly successful preachers, experience considerable difficulty in organizing their thought. It requires a logical and synthetic type of mind to do this, a type rarely combined with a mystical temperament, and with some disabilities here, and the demands of a busy pastorate, the time and work required to give the finishing touches to pulpit preparation have often, we fear, been neglected.

There is still another rather practical reason for this attitude of indifference. Almost every preacher has had to prepare an address on very short notice. He has put down on paper a few sentences, and has found his subject develop in such a way that he spoke as if inspired, and his message appeared to be very effective. On the other hand, he has prepared a sermon very carefully, bestowing upon it all the work that was necessary, as he thought, for its successful delivery, and his effort has been a miserable failure. Naturally, he asks: "What is the use of working hard on an outline?'' The reasons for success in one instance, however, and of apparent failure in the other, have their causes in something else than the outline. There are such causes as one's physical condition at the time of delivery; his mental attitude toward his subject, such as his conviction or the clearness with which he has thought it through; then there is the atmosphere of the meeting as effected by the preliminary exercises, the occasion, the responsiveness or otherwise of the audience, and the psychical condition too elusive to analyze. With all these factors operating, one can see how false the conclusion may be that the outline is the cause of failure or the lack of it the reason for one's success. It often happens, too, that when one selects a subject on short notice, he uses one with which he is very familiar, and the probable cause of success is not due so much to an unprepared outline as to the speaker's familiarity with his theme. Webster, when a discussion arose in the House, delivered a very powerful oration apparently without any preparation. He was afterwards complimented on his wonderful extemporaneous speech, to which he replied: ''Yes, it just took me twenty years to prepare it.'' No principles of homiletics have ever been discovered that guarantee a successful delivery every time one preaches.

But while we can not eliminate the possibility of failure, we can reduce it to a minimum. Incidentally it might be said that some of our worst failures are our greatest successes. A good outline is never the cause of failure in a sermon.

The value of a good outline can not be overestimated. It means that one has organized his thought, and that in itself should help to give confidence to the speaker and enable him to do his best under any circumstances. It gives to the speaker's utterance definiteness, directness and clearness of aim also, such as should lead to the orderly development and unfolding of his message. To have this feeling of preparedness multiplies indefinitely one's joy in preaching as well as the effectiveness of his work.

A clear outline relieves the speaker of the necessity of remembering the many details of his address. Instead of having to think of a great many ideas as if they were separate units, only held together by a very vague association, like marbles in a bag, all he has to remember is the three or four sentences which comprehend them, and in which each part of the discourse fits into its place. If the right principles of organization and development have been followed, there will be such a logical connection between the divisions that the conclusion of one will often suggest the next, and the same law of association and continuity will suggest, in turn, the particular development to be followed in each division. Such preaching releases more mental power for emphasizing each point, and thus aids concentration and vitality. A simple, logical, clear outline always makes the speaker's task easier than when the mind is burdened with endless minutia.

All that can be said for the benefit to the preacher can also be said for the gain to the hearer. Thought so presented will be easy to comprehend and retain. Is not this the great principle involved in the teaching of Jesus? He used simple illustrations of every-day life to which He gave a spiritual significance, so that the people could understand and remember it by the association He gave to it. He spoke of birds, lilies, seed, pearl, net, leaven, and these are the parts of His teaching we all remember the easiest. As one of the great preachers has said, He gave them "baskets" in which to carry away the spiritual food supplied them. In order for thought to be comprehended, it must be clear, and it can't be expressed clearly until it has been thought through. An outline should be statements well thought out and logically arranged, with the ideas grouped under such simple and expressive headings that by remembering two or three sentences the hearer can carry away all that has been said. They should be "baskets."

In a recent address before a university audience, a prominent speaker occupied half an hour discussing the subject of success. The address centered about two points, both of which were well developed and illustrated. First, he said that success was not the acquisition of material goods. Second, success was a useful life, faithfully lived. These two statements were so elaborated that all that was necessary to recall the whole address and its development was to remember these two sentences. For this reason it was very easy to comprehend and also to retain.

Having said this much as to the value of a good outline, an important question is: Should the outline of a sermon conform to any particular plan, and, if so, what is that plan? Among different exponents of the principles of homiletics there are differences of opinion as to the exact number of parts an outline ought to have, but all are agreed upon one essential point, and that is that there should be a logical beginning, middle and end. Phelps, in his work already quoted, gives to the sermon seven parts; viz., text, explanation, introduction, proposition, divisions, development and conclusion. Another very able writer on the same subject limits it to three parts: The introduction, development, conclusion. Both conform to the same idea, but Phelps gives a more elaborate analysis, and technically his form is preferable. Assuming that the sermon is based upon a text, it would naturally begin with an explanation of its setting, or, perhaps, where that is not necessary, an explanation of the text itself. Having done this, the next step would be to give the introduction to the subject, to show its importance, significance, or perhaps state the particular reason for bringing the subject to the notice of the people. This would then be followed by a statement of the specific aim or proposition that it is intended to demonstrate. Then would follow the divisions, the development and the conclusion. While technically correct, however, it has the disadvantage of being too elaborate for practical use, very few ministers attempting to observe all of these steps. On the other hand, the plan with only three parts is too general to be of any real service. The best form, and that which represents most nearly the plan of the best preachers, is the mean between these two extremes, and the aim of this work is to keep in mind not only such methods as are scientifically accurate, but also those that are most practicable. With this end in view, a good outline form is as follows: Theme and text, introduction, divisions, development and conclusion. This form avoids the difficulty of being too elaborate on the one hand, and of being too general on the other. A simple illustration of this form is given below in an outline which has been the basis of many a gospel sermon. It has captured the minds of many because of its simplicity, comprehensiveness and Scripturalness.

THE GOSPEL. Rom. 1:16.

Introduction.—Purpose of the sermon is to give a comprehensive view of the gospel, to see if it contains anything to be ashamed of.

I. FACTS—TO BE BELIEVED.

1. Death.
2. Burial.   } 1 Cor. 15:1-3.
3. Resurrection.

II. CONDITIONS—TO BE OBEYED.

1. Faith. Acts 16:31.
2. Repentance. Acts 2:38.
3. Confession. Rom. 10:9, 10.
4. Baptism. Acts 2:38.

III. PROMISES—TO BE ENJOYED.

1. Remission of sins. Acts 2:38.
2. Gift of the Holy Spirit. Acts 2:38.
3. Eternal life. John 3:16; Mark 16:16.

Conclusion.

Do you believe the facts?
Will you obey the commands?
If so, you will enjoy the promises.

The above arrangement is essential to every good sermon, with possibly one slight exception. It is not always necessary to have a text. A topic may

be used without it, and still conform to our definition of a sermon. A text is a very natural starting-
place, however, and also a very suitable way oftentimes of introducing the discussion of a theme. It
also has the value of linking up the preacher's message with a definite Scripture, and, if the explanation, interpretation or application of it be original,
whenever that passage of Scripture is read the hearer
will naturally associate it with the message he has
heard; while to preach without a text fails to give
the mind of the hearer this association of ideas. The
use of a text in preaching is an age-long practice
with many advantages, and ought not to be dispensed
with except on very rare occasions. The pulpit needs
to give the people more of the Bible, not less.

In this connection it may also be asked whether a
sermon may have a text and lack a theme. It may be
that instead of a theme being the genesis of a sermon,
a text may inspire it. In such a case it may be the
interpretation or explanation of the Scripture that
is the preacher's aim, but even if he has not stated
his theme in definite words, he should at least have a
clear idea of the point that he intends to make; he
should have a well-defined proposition. Wherever
there is this clear aim, some theme will be understood
even though not expressed. The other parts of the
outline, besides the subject and text, should appear
in every sermon, for no discourse is complete that
lacks any one of them.

With the six parts that we have suggested, the explanation of the text, the introduction and the proposition are all contracted into the introduction. To
use the term in this way widens its meaning some-

what, so as to include all that part of the sermon which precedes the discussion of the theme. There are three justifications for this change. In the first place, most preachers treat as introductory whatever precedes the actual discussion of the subject anyway, and nothing but formal technicalities will cause one to spend time treating them as separate units. Again, it frequently happens that one or other of these three parts included in the wider meaning of the term "introduction" is lacking from the sermon. There may not always be an explanation of the text. If there is no text, there can not be. If there is a text, it may be so simple as not to need explanation, or the explanation may be so closely related to the introduction of the subject itself that the differentiation may seem altogether arbitrary. Another practical reason for placing all that is said before the discussion under this one term is that this part of the sermon only requires a few sentences, occupying perhaps three or four minutes. It seems better, therefore, in the interests of freshness and variety, not to make an exact distinction of the steps involved in the preparation of the first few sentences. Freedom and spontaneity are needed here to get on good terms with the audience more than in any other part of the sermon.

The fourth part of the outline is the main divisions, or the headings under which the material of the sermon is organized. These are the most important parts of the outline, for the speaker depends on them to suggest to him the unfolding of his thought. When they are in such form as to do this, and at the same time are a digest or epitome of the sermon, they are a great aid to the speaker. More than this, the whole discussion or argument can only be retained by the hearer with any degree of clearness when the steps in the development are well stated. An example of making the main divisions stand out clearly, and their value in remembering the argument, may be seen from the following outline:

THE FOUR-SQUARE LIFE. Luke 2:52.

Introduction.—"In wisdom"—intelligence or mental development. "Stature"—physical development. "In favor with God"—spiritual development. "In favor with man"—moral development.

1. Any one of these faculties may degenerate.
2. To prevent degeneration conscious effort is necessary.
3. Effort put forth to develop a weak faculty may make that activity pleasurable.

Conclusion.—Appeal for full development, especially in regard to the highest part of our natures—the spiritual.

In the main divisions here used, there is suggested the material which would naturally be discussed in a theme of this kind. The progressive character of the three statements causes one division to prepare the way and in some measure suggest the next, and so it makes it easy for the preacher to recall his thought, and equally easy for the hearer also to remember what is said. The importance of this part of the outline will thus be obvious. No matter how well informed one may be on any subject, his information is of little value either to himself or others until he has organized it and given clear expression to his divisions. Unless a speaker has carried out this mental process, his ideas are like a picture out of focus; we have a kind of vague, general conception of what he is trying to say, but we don't get the relation of his facts to each other, and his work is only half done. There is in the statement of the main divisions excellent opportunity for showing ability and for clarifying the main purpose.

The next part of the outline is its development. In detail this will be treated in the chapter on this topic; here our interest is only in the form of it. This part of the sermon is sometimes spoken of as subdivisions, although this term rather has reference to a tabulation of the ideas under the main headings. You might have subdivisions without much development of the theme, but an orderly development requires subdivisions. For the time being, however, we may consider these two terms as synonymous. The development should be a logical working out of the main divisions in the same way as the main divisions are related to the proposition. In the subdivisions symbols are generally used, either figures or letters. It is quite immaterial which method is employed; that is the best which helps most to distinguish the main ideas from those that are subsidiary, and for this purpose some employ figures and others letters. In the sermons of many able preachers the use of any symbols for subdivisions is omitted; as, *e. g.*, in Maclaren's "Expositions," while Spurgeon rarely failed to use the other plan. For those who speak from brief notes the symbolic method has much to commend it, but would not have the same value for those who write their sermons in full. An outline with divisions and subdivisions has already been given in the sermon on "The Gospel."

The last part of the outline is the conclusion. Its place and importance are universally recognized. The methods to be employed to make it effective will be considered in the chapter on that topic.

Another matter of interest is, How much should one put into his notes for use in the pulpit? This depends upon the man, the subject, and his mastery of it. Some acquire the habit early in their public work of speaking without notes, and there can be no question about this being the ideal method. It gives greater opportunity for the expression of personality, inspires confidence in one's message, and makes it easier to hold the attention. For the great majority of men, however, who preach regularly to the same congregations, this plan is not practicable. In general, a preacher using manuscript should have just as many notes as are necessary to bring to his mind the content of his sermon. In many cases abbreviations and keywords can be used. If the development of the sermon is by illustration, a very brief statement will suffice to recall the thought. On the other hand, a doctrinal theme, involving Scripture references, quotations or statements of fact, will usually require more elaborate and careful statement. Even here, however, if one can quote his references from memory, and is familiar with his facts, considerable abbreviation is possible. So that if one's preaching comprehends different types of sermons (as it ought to do), the amount of manuscript used will be determined both by his subject and the extent to which he has assimilated it.

QUESTIONS ON CHAPTER II.

1. Should it ever be necessary for a preacher to be disappointed in his sermon?

2. Explain why a good outline is an aid to success in preaching.

3. Is it desirable to take the sermon outline into the pulpit?

4. What causes are chiefly responsible for preaching without texts?

5. Why must a sermon almost necessarily have a theme, even though it has its origin in the explanation of some text?

6. What justification is there for regarding all the sermon material that precedes the main divisions as the introduction?

7. Why should the main divisions of a sermon be clearly stated?

8. What are the chief reasons that account for the lack of main divisions or the bad statement of them?

9. What advantages are there in using symbols for the subdivisions of a sermon?

10. Describe the process of preparing a sermon outline.

CHAPTER III.

THE THEME

IN the preceding chapter the first part of a sermon was designated the theme. As there are several terms that have very similar meanings, a distinction may here be made between them, and then hereafter they will be used with the significance given. The general topic of a sermon is its subject. Illustrations of this would be "Faith" or "The Resurrection." When we take some phase of a subject, and discuss it in a limited sense, as is the case in practically every good sermon, it becomes the theme. Thus faith, as a general subject, may be restricted to "The Venture of Faith," or "The Resurrection" may be confined to "The Significance of the Resurrection," both of which modifications would change these subjects into *themes*. Now, having decided to preach on one or other of these themes, it is important that there should be a definite aim, some particular point that the preacher wishes to make. Thus, with the theme, "The Venture of Faith," he may wish to show that faith is necessary to any great achievement in life, or he might discuss "The Significance of the Resurrection" in such a way as to demonstrate that belief in the resurrection of Jesus is fundamental to the Christian faith. This statement of the aim of the discourse becomes the *proposition*. So that the general topic is the subject, the special phase of it which forms the title of the sermon is the theme, and the specific point to be worked out in the discussion is the proposition.

In determining the character of a preacher's theme many influences are at work. No two men express themselves alike. No two men would use the same material, even though preaching on the same theme. This is due to the different elements that constitute their personalities, and no two men are the same. In the background of every life are one's temperament, training and experience, and these factors very largely determine the material of his message, and in a large measure his subject also. As one prepares to face his congregation, the ever-recurring question is: "What shall I preach about?" Then, perhaps unconsciously, he decides upon some topic which is suggested by his experience or the environment in which he lives.

Perhaps the chief influence determining the preacher's theme is the *needs of the congregation* as he understands them. Any man who has upon his heart the moral and spiritual welfare of the people will naturally seek first of all in his preaching to bring to them a message that will help them in their difficulties and perplexities, as well as to strengthen and stimulate them in their nobler aspirations. Perhaps ministers as a whole fail to realize as they ought the needs of many of those who come to church seeking help and encouragement. Only when we preach a sermon that has found a particularly responsive note in some life do we appreciate this fact. In every service there are those who are yearning for something beyond the capacity of this present life to supply.

They are anxiously longing to have the unseen and the eternal made more real to their daily lives. They are in a very real sense hungering for the "bread of life." If we could but exercise our imaginations and see men and women at their daily tasks, oftentimes handicapped by exacting duties, sometimes struggling against sickness or financial embarrassment, or if we could but know the mental life of those who are meeting with continual disappointment in their undertakings, and sometimes perplexed in mind or grieved at heart—if, I say, we could see all this, would not the needs of our congregations stir us more deeply as we contemplate the preparation of our sermons? And yet this is no exaggeration of human life as it is. Then, there are those who are seeking to give some larger expression to their lives, who need something more satisfying, something that will give them a better interpretation of existence. For all of this the preacher has the remedy if he rightly divides the word of God and does not feed the people on the husks of speculation or answer their longings by merely gratifying the æsthetic or moral natures. The people, somehow, instinctively feel that the only remedy for their deepest needs is to be found in religion. The soul cries out for God, and while, through music, literature, and the ideals of social service, one may approach the higher or spiritual nature, fundamentally these things no more satisfy the longings of the soul than a good book will the physical appetite. The needs of the people should be upon the heart of every man as he prepares his sermon, and perhaps in the life of Jesus we have a suggestion of the way this can be done, for He was found where the burdens were, in order that He might help to lift them. Willingness to seek and ability to feel the needs of human life are the prerequisites to the right approach to the preparation of a helpful sermon.

Having noted the needs of the people, the next factor to consider influencing the selection of a theme is *temperament*. The man of the optimistic type, and every man ought to be, will seek to encourage the people in the ways of righteousness in spite of the materialistic influences that surround them, and even if some members of the congregation are indifferent to their opportunities and obligations, he will endeavor to strengthen the faithful. The man of the pessimistic or negative type will allow himself to become depressed over the situation, and will complainingly and discouragingly remind his congregation of the evil characteristics of our age, and his discourses will point more to the sin of worldliness than to encouragement in faithfulness. No one can ever hope to help his people very much by negative preaching, and of all types the pessimistic is most out of place in the pulpit because it misrepresents the whole genius of Christianity. It is a spirit alien to the gospel, which is fundamentally "good news."

Of those, however, whose preaching is positive in character, there are different temperaments. There is the man of learning whose chief interest is in books, in ideas, rather than in people. Because of what he is, his sermon themes are likely to find their expression in doctrinal and argumentative subjects, or, perhaps, in explaining the problems of life in a philosophical way. His messages may be models of literary beauty, since they are largely illustrated by choice quotations from great writers. Such discourses, because they deal with but one phase of life, will only reach a small percentage in any congregation. Even in America it has to be remembered that college graduates only represent about three per cent. of the population, and many very good and able men are failing to reach a large part of the community because they have no message for the lives of about 97 per cent. of the people. Then, there is the emotional temperament. The man of this type will get nearer to the hearts of the people and will express himself in themes that are aglow with feeling. In doing so he will only meet the needs of a part of his congregation also. In general, it may be said that the majority enjoy sermons better that have the emotional appeal than those that are intellectual, but the fully trained mind should have "power to think, power to feel and power to will." It is probably true, however, that most preachers are either too intellectual or too emotional, and, in order to make sure that there is food in one's sermons for all mental groups represented in the congregation, it is well for a preacher to take an occasional inventory of his sermons, and see if there is sufficient variety to meet the needs of all the congregation. The different books of the Bible and the texts selected will be a reasonably good indication of the tendency of one's pulpit efforts.

Another factor exercising a considerable influence in the selection of themes is the preacher's *experience*. One's illustrations will naturally be taken from the environment in which he lives or has lived. If he has been connected with industrial life and addresses industrial people, the problems of capital and labor will oftentimes form the background of his thinking, and sometimes even become more directly a part of his messages. Preaching by those who live in industrial centers, and whose work and conversation are chiefly with working people, is often noticed to take on a tinge of socialism. This is a perfectly natural result of environmental conditions.

Those whose life-work has been in centers of learning frequently indicate by their pulpit utterances the intellectual struggle through which they have passed, or through which they are seeking to guide others. So their themes will be largely colored by struggles against doubt, or efforts to bring into harmony apparent conflicts between science and religion.

Another phase of life's experience that sometimes finds expression is the sorrow or grief that has entered into one's life. To give a testimony on rare occasions to the help one has received from his faith in a dark hour, is perfectly natural and proper. A preacher addresses himself to a very sympathetic group of people, but there are two ways in which one may refer to the sorrows of his life which are entirely out of place. One is to make such frequent mention of them that the people begin to suspect that the references made are not caused by tender feeling or affectionate remembrance, so much as a desire for effect. Any audience will deeply resent any such impropriety. The other danger to one who has passed through or lives under a cloud is to select depressing topics, or to preach with "tears in his voice." Such preaching is neither inspiring, helpful nor wholesome. The yoke of Christ is intended to enable us to bear our burdens, and such an attitude indicates that the preacher himself is not wearing the yoke. Preachers need to preach on positive, helpful, uplifting and inspiring themes, rising above their own sorrows and misfortunes, just as Jesus, almost under the shadow of the cross, staggering under the burden of His own grief, said to His disciples: "Let not your hearts be troubled: believe in God, believe also in me." Our past has become a part of ourselves; we can not separate ourselves from it or eliminate it. Just as it was put into the mouth of Ulysses to say after his journeyings, "I am a part of all that I have met," so this past experience of ours becomes the basis for the interpretation of the present, but we must be careful to suppress those elements of our experience which mar our hopefulness and cheerfulness, and, consequently, affect the efficiency of our work.

The last point to be noted among the factors determining the theme is the preacher's own *conception of religious truth*. Modern religious training produces men with very different interpretations of Christianity. This means really that it is a part of experience, but the specific character of that experience seems to merit a separate treatment of the topic. If one's view of the Bible is such that he regards it as the authoritative word of God, his themes will glow with assurance, confidence and hope. He will select themes with a positive rather than a philosophical outlook, and he will discuss them with that definiteness with which they are presented in the Scriptures, and make no apology for his attitude. On the other hand, if he does not know what he believes, or is not sure that he believes anything at all, he will be very likely to give the people a review of his own nightmares, as Dr. Chapman has well expressed it; or else will seek topics for discussion that are only indirectly connected with the field of religion. So that if two preachers both analyzed the needs of the people, and it were humanly possible for them to have the same temperament and experience, and they both decided to preach on the same theme, the two different views of religious truth would determine an entirely different treatment of the subject. So that it may be said that in so far as one is able to understand the needs of the people, control his temperament, enrich his experience, and get the right view of Christian truth, he will increase his capacity for successful preaching.

What, now, are the characteristics of a good theme? Are there any principles that can be applied that will help one to determine beforehand whether or not his message will be well received? Without doubt the first essential of a good theme is that it must have a *vital interest*. In other words, it must be closely related to life. There is a Christian interpretation or ideal for every phase of human activity. In the physical realm we are taught that our bodies are temples of the Holy Spirit. Every form of licentiousness, dissipation, or even recreation that destroys the usefulness and efficiency of the human body, is contrary to the Christian program of life. This principle is capable of unlimited application, as it applies to all our physical life. In the social sphere we are to be guided by the principle of helpfulness, or to reflect in that realm the ideal of a Christian personality. Such a standard will not only determine the character of our social life, but will also limit its extent and decide the purpose for which it is sought. It will proscribe certain forms of pleasure, it will give to others a new interpretation, and point out

41

limitations even to the most healthful recreations. In the realm of thought there is no thinking that is unrelated to God. All serious thinking on man's relation to the universe in which he finds himself is related to the great problems of life, death, immortality, sin and holiness. These are topics that never grow old; they only await new and interesting ways of presenting and applying them. People can be stirred as much to-day as ever on these great themes so long as the discussion of them does not end in a question mark. Any audience will listen with delight to sermons on the brevity and uncertainty of human life, if the darkness be taken away from the tomb. Immortality can still be shown to be the universal craving, although speculations always fail to satisfy, while Christ's statement, "I am come that ye might have life," still awakens hope in every human heart, and His promise, "He that believeth in me, though he were dead, yet shall he live," is still the only light for souls in darkness. Sin can still be shown to be the universal experience of the human race. Though fools may laugh at it, and philosophers explain it away, it remains an undeniable fact that "all have sinned." Why does the sense of fear creep over dying souls? Surely the sting of death is sin, and when sin is taken away there is no sting in death. Holiness is not a dream, nor the obsession of a misguided fancy. It is still the aspiration of earth's noblest souls, the highest satisfaction in life and the greatest consolation in death. Any great theme must touch life, but the preacher has to find the application and discover new ways of presentation.

A good theme must also have a *clear aim*. One must not only talk on his subject, but must talk to a point. Sometimes the title of the sermon may indicate one's aim, but whether it does or not there should always be some definite objective. This is usually spoken of as the proposition, or the statement of the particular truth to be demonstrated. It should be possible for the aim of each sermon to be definitely stated in one sentence. If this can not be done, the preacher is either discussing generalities or else it is a sign that he has not thought his subject through. Sometimes it may not be desirable to state the aim. One may have a goal before him that would awaken prejudice if stated at the beginning of his discourse, and perhaps it is better to conceal the proposition from the audience until he has won them over to his arguments. It should always be true, however, no matter what the occasion or subject, that the preacher have clearly in mind the end he wishes to reach, whether he states it in his discourse or not. It is characteristic of the sermons referred to in the New Testament that they were delivered with the purpose in mind of getting the people to make a decision. They were intended to accomplish something very definitely, and so, on the day of Pentecost, they said: "Brethren, what shall we do?" Again we read: "When they believed Philip preaching good tidings concerning the kingdom of God and the name of Jesus Christ, they were baptized, both men and women." Philip preached Jesus unto the Ethiopian and baptized him into Christ before he left him. When some definite purpose inspires the sermon, the material is collected and organized with that end in view, and the message has a directness of approach and appeal for which there is much precedent in the New Testament. You can't hit a target if you don't have one, and it is likewise a psychological impossibility to accomplish anything definitely with a sermon that has no clear point or aim.

A further characteristic of a good theme is that it be *positive in form.* To announce as the title of a sermon, "Does God Exist?" "Did Jesus Rise from the Dead?" "Is the Bible Inspired?" or "Has the Church Failed?" has at the basis a false idea. The reason for the interrogatory form is to arouse curiosity by the preacher's non-committal of himself to the subject. No one, however, reading these sermon titles doubts for one minute the attitude that will be taken up by him. He knows that an effort will be made to demonstrate that God does exist, that Jesus did rise from the dead, that the Bible is inspired, and that the church has not failed. Furthermore, there is always a danger of suggesting doubt. Many will probably read the announcement who will not hear the sermon, and even a hint of the possibility of the fundamentals of Christianity not being true, is unwise. The statement of the themes in the form given above also has another disadvantage in that it is likely to cause a discussion of the subject in which objections to Christianity are presented. To logically discuss the subject would almost demand this kind of treatment. There are always dangers here. In an effort to be fair, one may state objections that his reply may fail to remove, and thus leave the people with doubts that they did not have before the sermon, and most people have enough misgivings of their own forced upon them by their unbelieving associates in the busy, every-day world, or by circumstances, and ought not to have these augmented when they come to hear the gospel. The people expect Christian truth to be defended in the pulpit, and, from the standpoint of the attractiveness of the theme, it would be much better to give a positive statement of the subjects involved by saying, ''Reasons for Believing in God,'' or to make it personal and say, ''Why I Believe in God,'' ''Proofs of the Resurrection,'' ''Why I Believe in the Bible,'' and ''Triumphs of the Church.'' When put into such form one can logically discuss his theme without ''doubtful disputations,'' and those who are troubled with doubts can get what they want when they come to church; namely, positive demonstrations of Christian truth and interpretations of life in harmony with them. The pulpit has too often been used as a place where the preacher has paraded his own doubts. It is not necessary for him to exalt doubt or to trouble the congregation with any misgivings he may have in order to prove his mental sincerity. Even Hume, whose skeptical attitude regarding the fundamentals of Christianity is so well known, used to go to hear the very orthodox Rowland Hill preach, and, when taunted by friends for his inconsistency, he said that he wanted to hear some one preach who had convictions. Preachers miss the mark when they think that subjects suggesting doubt are attractive to those whose minds are really disturbed. The world is yearning for a positive message from the pulpit on the fundamentals of Christianity. Most people have enough doubts of their own.

In the life of the preacher there is no problem more regular in its appearance, nor more insistent in its demand, than the question, ''What shall I preach about next Sunday?'' He is compelled to come before the people at the appointed time with a sermon, whether he has had an inspiration or not. The difficulty in sermonizing has to be frankly admitted, that it takes a very brilliant man to produce two fresh, vital, original messages every week. Indeed, it takes a genius to do this, and there are not very many of these men either in the pulpit or out of it. There are, however, some aids which reduce the perplexity of the problem. A very fruitful method of getting suggestions for sermon topics is the *intensive study of individual books of the Bible.* The value of this suggestion is not only a deep conviction from personal experience, but is also the testimony of many able preachers.

The treasures of the Scriptures are most prized when we discover them for ourselves, for they then become ours in a very real sense. This method not only gives an ever-flowing stream of suggestions for pulpit material, but is also a splendid discipline for one's own devotional life, as it systematically builds up his Biblical knowledge, gives him a deeper appreciation of the Scriptures, and enriches all his religious experience. It really makes his interpretations of the word of God the expression of his own soul, because their truths are interwoven into his daily life. Those who have given this plan a fair trial, apart altogether from this helpful discipline, have found it surprisingly fruitful in sermonic suggestion. It is also an avenue to that most desirable of all pulpit work—the popular exposition of the Scriptures. The fact is that people know a great deal about the Bible, but do not know the contents of the Book itself, and will always welcome explanations or applications of the text when made in a clear, vital and interesting way. This method of intensive study should commend itself to all who desire to be good students of the Word, interesting preachers, or strong Christian characters.

Another very helpful way of discovering sermon themes, and also material, is to be found in one's daily experience. Conversations with those who tell of their joy in Christian service, confessions of those who are not Christians, but who express a longing for a better life, all suggest approaches to themes of universal value. What we see in life depends, of course, on what we are. A party of tourists were being shown over some old castles in Spain, when one of the number remarked to another, "Hasn't this been a tiresome day?" The person addressed observed to some friends afterwards that to him it was one of the most enjoyable days of his life. The cultivation of one's powers of *observation,* and the ability to seize upon those elements in conversation that have moral and spiritual significance, are great achievements.

Beyond these two suggestions there are no technical rules that will furnish one with a supply of themes for sermons. The increase in the rate at which topics will suggest themselves is, in the final analysis, proportionate to the growth of the man. While the young preacher may have some difficulties in the early part of his ministry, he will find that as his horizon broadens by regular habits of study and Christian service, these difficulties will disappear. The poorest solution of the problem is for a man, when he changes his location, to depend on old sermons. By so doing the ability to discover and use the new and original material weakens, and, if continued too long, one loses the power to grow and reaches what has been termed the "ministerial dead-line."

Before closing this chapter it might be of value to say a few words on the matter of advertising one's themes. For those who are preaching regularly to the same congregation, there is little advantage in announcing sermon topics. Only on such occasions as there is a subject which is known to be of special interest is there any need for such an announcement to be made, as perhaps in a series of sermons, in the discussion of some current event, or when some matter affecting the congregation's program of work is under consideration. Largely it depends upon local circumstances and upon the theme's importance.

What characteristics should sermons possess, however, in order to attract people through advertising? There are two plans that can be used with advantage. One of these is to *excite curiosity*. This may be done by concealing the material that is to be discussed. "Strange Ways of Accomplishing Great Ends" is the title of a sermon on the fall of Jericho. It illustrates the point, although it is rather an awkward statement. Recently a sermon was preached at an opportune moment on "The Minority Report," based upon the words of Isa. 53:1, "Who hath believed our report?" The appeal to curiosity is a legitimate way of gaining interest, and is rarely carried too far. There is a danger, however, and care should be taken not to disappoint people with a commonplace discussion after awakening anticipations of hearing something unusual and striking, for they are only caught that way once.

The other method that can be used to call special attention to a sermon is to announce a *subject that is interesting in itself*. Such subjects at special times and places as "The Unpardonable Sin," "Divine Healing," "The Second Coming," "The Sabbath," "Where Are the Righteous Dead?" and similar topics, belong to this class. The matter of making a special feature of advertising belongs more to the field of evangelism, or protracted meetings, than to the ordinary work of the pulpit, although it is to be noted that practically all popular preachers do advertise nearly all, if not all, of their sermon themes. The public mind, however, has grown accustomed to expecting from evangelists something unusual in matter as well as in methods. There is no reason why the plan that brings a crowd occasionally should not be used continuously, except that it requires a genius to keep it up. There is always the danger, of course, in popular advertising of religious services, of compromising good taste and lowering the dignity of the pulpit. Really big men never fall into this error. It is true that for some centers, where the cultural standard of the community is not very high, extraordinary messages and methods of approach are sometimes justifiable. It is always well, however, to reflect upon Jesus' method. He worked among the masses, and He reached them. They heard Him gladly. He used the common things of every-day life for illustrations, but there is no instance where the Saviour's words have any suggestion of vulgarity, or where they fall below the level of good taste. To speak simply is a fine art, and a worthy aim of any preacher, but the lewd, the coarse and the vulgar are out of place and unworthy of any public man, and, most of all, in the preacher of the gospel. Any clear-headed student of Jesus' manner and method can not go far wrong.

1. What is necessary in order to a proper understanding of the spiritual needs of a congregation?

2. What are some of the things that determine the temperament of a preacher?

3. How can one enrich his experience for preaching?

4. Are negative themes ever justifiable?

5. What elements in sermon material vitalize it most?

6. Why is a definite proposition necessary in order to effective preaching?

7. State the theme of a sermon, and then give its proposition.

8. What must a preacher do in order to get sermon material that will really help people?

9. Give an illustration, other than those mentioned in the book, of a sermon that is interesting in itself, and also one that is attractive, but conceals the nature of the discussion.

CHAPTER IV.

THE TEXT

ONE of the interesting things in the history of preaching is the use that has been made of texts. In the Jewish synagogue the discourses consisted of explanations of the Old Testament Scriptures. We have some examples of this brought before us in the record of the work of Jesus and His apostles. In the fourth chapter of Luke we read: "And Jesus came to Nazareth, where he had been brought up: and he entered as his custom was, into the synagogue on the sabbath day, and stood up to read. And there was delivered unto him the book of the prophet Isaiah. And he opened the book, and found the place where it was written,

The Spirit of the Lord is upon me,

Because he anointed me to preach good tidings to the poor:

He hath sent me to proclaim release to the captives,

And recovering of sight to the blind,

To set at liberty them that are bruised,

To proclaim the acceptable year of the Lord.

And he closed the book, and gave it back to the attendant, and sat down, and the eyes of all in the synagogue were fastened on him. And he began to say unto them, To-day hath this scripture been fulfilled in your ears." Again, in Acts 13:14ff., we read: Paul and his company, "passing through from Perga, came to

Antioch of Pisidia; and they went into the synagogue on the sabbath day, and sat down. And after the reading of the law and the prophets the rulers of the synagogue sent unto them, saying, Brethren, if ye have any word of exhortation for the people, say on.'' Then Paul began a discourse in which he explained from the law and the prophets the Messiahship of Jesus.

In the early Christian assemblies they probably had discussions or exhortations based upon the words of Jesus and the apostles. We read that ''they continued stedfastly in the apostles' teaching'' (Acts 2:42). Several of these short talks were very likely given on each occasion they met (see Col. 3:16; Eph. 5:19). The references to the services in the Scripture would also indicate that they were informal. There were no trained preachers, and each contributed what he could to the upbuilding of the congregation. In the later development of the services of the church, topical and more formal preaching became the rule. The reformers, however, in their zeal to restore to the people the Bible, introduced the method of using a text as the basis of the sermon, and this method has persisted as a general practice down to our own day.

There has been a tendency in modern times to depart from this plan. This has been brought about very largely by the changed view concerning the function of the pulpit. Religion has a vital connection with all of life's activities, whether social, political, economic or educational, and because of this some preachers have come to regard the pulpit as a fit place to discuss problems belonging to these fields. It is quite evident that such discourses do not need a text, and

52

that generally the use of one would be in such an accommodated sense as to indicate that it was merely used for the sake of form. In such circumstances the natural thing to do is to dispense with the text altogether rather than adhere rigidly to a form.

Another influence, perhaps, which has a tendency to do away with the use of texts is the tendency to topical preaching. In earlier days it was not necessary to advertise sermon subjects. When Sunday came round people went to church as a matter of course. All that was necessary for the preacher to do was to announce his text, and then explain and develop it. But times have changed. In these days it is often necessary to draw congregations, and to do this alluring topics are advertised and extraordinary methods adopted. This effort to reach people who are indifferent to religion has led to a change of emphasis in preaching from the text to the topic, and, while many attractive themes have texts to suggest them, the tendency to neglect the use of texts continues.

The practical test, however, is the one that should decide the matter. Can any more good be accomplished by employing texts than by omitting them? What advantages are to be gained, if any, by using texts at all? In the first place, the Bible is a recognized source of truth, and so a quotation from the Scripture gives authority to one's message. The Bible has always stood in a class by itself. Its teachings are entitled to consideration above the teachings of any other book. When a preacher offers his own explanations of truth, without giving them a Scriptural basis, we feel justified in accepting or rejecting them, the same as we would if we were listening to the views of a speaker on any other subject. When, however, he can show that he is explaining or emphasizing what is taught in the Bible, we feel that his message is entitled to more thoughtful and respectful consideration.

Then, again, many of the texts of Scripture express spiritual truth in such form as to help in making the message effective. Very often a text serves as an epitome of the whole sermon. Not only does it give the thought, but it often expresses it in language that is clear, forceful and euphonious, apart altogether from any authority we may attach to it because of its source. All scholars are agreed about the literary value of the Bible. The marvel is that schools and colleges, where literary models are presented and studied, have failed for so long a time to use it more as a text-book. There are no better literary forms to be found any-where, and no more elevating ideals in any literature. If it were not the word of God, but the word of man only, its inherent literary worth would preserve it from decay.

In some texts we have the most vital subjects presented in such simplicity and rhythmic beauty as to be long remembered after the sermon is forgotten. Who, in preaching about sin, could find words more universally true, or more expressive, than those in the Book of Romans: "All have sinned and fall short of the glory of God" (3:23). This fact is enshrined in the customs and rites of all peoples. In speaking of the character of God, no words will ever be found that will be more attractive than John 3:16: "God so loved the world, that he gave his only begotten Son, that whosoever believeth on him should not perish, but have eternal life." No words of comfort will ever be found that will come closer to the human heart than those of the twenty-third Psalm, "The Lord is my shepherd, I shall not want," or the words of Jesus in John 14:1-3: "Let not your heart be troubled: believe in God, believe also in me." In other words, practically every truth that we wish to express, of a religious character, may be conveyed through passages of Scripture. If we can impress the text, even though what we say in elaboration is forgotten, we have caused it to have permanent value for the lives of the hearers.

Another great value growing out of the use of texts is the wonderful power of association, of giving to the mind a way of remembering our messages. Long after the sermons are forgotten the texts used are remembered. That does not mean that all that was said is lost, but rather means that the discussion gave meaning to the text. Those who have been interested in spiritual things for a long time will have little difficulty in recalling sermons heard years ago, although all that is remembered is the text. A man once told the writer that he had not been to church for twenty-five years, yet he could repeat the text of a sermon he heard, and state the place in the Bible where it could be found. Now, what would have happened to that message if it had not been linked up with a passage of Scripture? But there is even more than the recollection of the substance of the sermon involved in this association. We often connect with the message the man who gave it, and so our lives are enriched by the memory of his personality. To elaborate, explain or apply a passage of Scripture so as to impress people is to give it a meaning that will remain with them all through their lives.

55

From the preacher's standpoint, also, there are homiletical advantages to be gained by using a text. It very often helps the introduction of a sermon by making an easy approach to the theme. Sometimes subjects that are more or less difficult and delicate can be introduced in this way. This is true, for example, in a series of sermons where subjects that it would be otherwise difficult to introduce can be mentioned because they are connected with others in the group. Such series as the Ten Commandments have been used in this way in modern times. Missions and stewardship are also topics whose introduction is made easier when a text is used at the beginning. Every phase of modern life has its application in the gospel, and every evil has there its sole remedy. For this reason no theme of a religious character is without a starting-point in some passage of Scripture.

A text not only aids in the introduction of a sermon, however, but also in its development. It helps to give a directness of aim, and to describe the field within which the development is to be carried on. This limitation of scope tends to more intensive study of the theme, and also assists in eliminating irrelevant material.

Perhaps, however, one of the greatest advantages of all is that the use of texts familiarizes the people with the Bible. When done well, nothing is more interesting than the reading, explaining and interpreting of the Scriptures. When we can tell the people something about a text that they don't know, or illustrate it in some new way, or make an application of it never before heard, putting life and power into the message, there is no public utterance on any question, in any realm, given under any circumstances, that is more interesting and helpful. Above all, it is not by any wisdom of our own, but only as we give the people the word of God, that we can hope to "make them wise unto salvation through faith which is in Christ Jesus."

A discriminating use needs to be made of Scripture texts, however, for all passages do not have the same value, nor can they all be used in the same way. One type that needs to be used with discretion is the interpolated text. A preacher knowing a text to be of this character ought not to use it as the sole doctrinal basis of a sermon, even though the people being addressed may not know that it belongs to this category. If some one happened to be in the audience who did know that it was regarded as an interpolation, and the passage were not qualified, he would probably lose confidence in the preacher's scholarship for all time, or, if he had a suspicion that the preacher did know, he might lose confidence in the man himself, which would be more serious. If, on the other hand, he did mention the fact that the passage did not appear in some of the earlier manuscripts of the Bible, probably a large portion of his audience would not understand the problem involved, and it would only weaken their confidence in the authority of the Scriptures. What, then, is the sanest way of dealing with such passages? Take, for example, Acts 8:37, which is of such doubtful repute that it is omitted altogether from the Revised Version of the New Testament. Here we have Philip's question and the eunuch's reply before his baptism. It is the only instance in New Testament conversion where a direct confession of faith is recorded before baptism.

Is it legitimate to quote this? Yes, if given as an illustration of the passage of undoubted authority in Rom. 10:9, 10, which says: "If thou shalt *confess with thy mouth* Jesus as Lord, and shalt believe in thy heart that God raised him from the dead, thou shalt be saved: for with the heart man believeth unto righteousness; and *with the mouth* confession is made unto salvation." This passage of Scripture completely covers the point, and the passage in Acts 8:37 can be quoted in connection with it without making any reference to the matter of its being an interpolation. This method enables the preacher to be true to his own conscience, and at the same time prevents his scholarship from falling under suspicion.

There are other passages of Scripture where we have the record of the words of uninspired men. Such, for example, are the words of Eliphaz, Bildad and Zophar, in their conversations with Job, in which they express sentiments that never were true, and are arguing against righteous Job. In the epilogue of the book, Jehovah, addressing Eliphaz, says: "My wrath is kindled against thee, and against thy two friends; for ye have not spoken of me the thing that is right, as my servant Job hath." Thus, in quoting words of any of these three men, one might be presenting as truth that which the Book later labels as falsehood. It is evident, upon making a study of many isolated passages which belong to this class, that many of them may be useful so long as the character and circumstances of the speakers are noted. Agrippa said to Paul: "With but little persuasion thou wouldst fain make me a Christian" (Acts 26:28). Now, Agrippa was a heathen, and may either have made this remark ironically or sin-

cerely. It matters little as to his religious outlook, or
even the spirit in which these words were uttered, so
far as their value for a text is concerned. One's personal opinion on this matter may help to make an
interesting introduction, but the text can be used to
appeal to those who are hesitating in the matter of accepting the gospel regardless of the state of Agrippa's
mind when he gave utterance to these words. It is
well, nevertheless, to discriminate clearly between inspired words and those that were never intended to be
inspired, and which may even be false. "The king's
business requireth haste" may be used in an accommodated sense, as is the case in a modern religious song,
but in the setting in which it occurs in the Scripture
it is a falsehood, and really reflects upon the character
of the speaker.

Sometimes a passage of Scripture may convey only
a part of the truth on a subject, and, when used alone,
may give a one-sided view. In such cases it is well to
associate with it parallel passages in order to complete
the idea. An example of this would be Gal. 6:2, "Bear
ye one another's burdens." Another verse (6:5) says,
"Every man must bear his own burden." The one em-
phasizes the obligation of Christians to each other in
their corporate relationship; the other, the inevitable
weight that every man must bear himself, no matter
how willing others may be to help him. Even a third
text might be added to these, which says, "Cast your
burden upon the Lord" (Ps. 55:22), which expresses
the divine help in time of trouble. A consideration of
all three of these aspects is necessary in discussing the
matter of burden-bearing, otherwise the subject might
be dealt with in such a way as to make a man think

that other Christians ought to bear his burdens for him,
or make him depressed by thinking he has to bear them
all alone, or yet to cause him to ignore them, inasmuch
as the Lord has asked us to cast them upon Him.
To use a combination of texts when such a situation is
presented is always legitimate, and often very desirable.
It may sometimes happen, however, that the use of
parallel texts this way may widen the field too much
to give to the sermon the particular emphasis we want
to make. It may be our desire, for example, to limit
the subject of burden-bearing to ''The Personal Aspect
of Burden-bearing,'' or ''Mutual Responsibility in Burden-bearing,'' or ''Divine Help in Burden-bearing.''
Where a limitation of the subject is thus made, and it
is only intended to use one of them as the theme, it
may often help the situation by mentioning the other
aspects of the subject. This enables people to see that
one's thinking has a correct relationship to cognate
texts and facts, and that one has not become obsessed
with one idea to the exclusion of other points of view.
This also helps to inspire confidence in one's judgment
and emphasis of life, and thereby gains more respectful
consideration for his opinions.

Another type is the abbreviated or incomplete
text. Dr. Chapman's sermon, ''And Peter,'' and
Spurgeon's sermon, given later, ''As and So,'' are
types of this class. Generally speaking, such abbreviated passages are not good. There may be rare
occasions when a genius can defy rules and principles,
but geniuses are rare, and so are the occasions when
they can do this. These abbreviated passages do not
mean anything at all as they are stated. Shakespeare,
Milton, and possibly a few others with giant intellects,

may violate the fundamental laws of grammar and rhetoric occasionally, but lesser lights find it more to their advantage to work in harmony with those laws. When one is convinced that he is a Spurgeon, a Moody, a Chapman, or a Maclaren, and that the unusual occasion has arrived, it will be safe for him to use these ungrammatical and incomplete texts; till then the alternate method may be more desirable.

In contrast to this class there is another kind at the other extreme—long texts. A preacher once announced that his text was to be found in 1 Tim. 3:16: "And without controversy great is the mystery of godliness;

He who was manifested in the flesh,
   Justified in the spirit,
      Seen of angels,
Preached among the nations,
   Believed on in the world,
      Received up in glory."

Usually such texts are unwise for several reasons. In the first place, they are too long to be remembered, so that they do not serve as an epitome of the discourse. In the next place, such texts are too extensive; they cover too much territory to allow for unusual development by intensive study. Any one of the six things mentioned in this verse would be broad enough alone in its scope to justify a whole sermon. Another disadvantage of a long text is that instead of arousing a feeling of anticipation, as it ought to do, there is frequently a sensation akin to that of anticipated punishment on the part of the younger members of the congregation, and, perhaps, it may not be altogether untrue to say that this sensation is shared in part by the older people also.

Coming now to the more positive side of the discussion on texts, let us enquire what constitutes a good text for a sermon. The value of different passages of Scripture varies, of course, with different individuals, because of the difference in their temperament and training. Any one may write down for himself ten or twelve of his favorite passages, and then look for the particular quality in them that is the cause of his appreciation, and such an introspection will bring its own reward. There are, however, some passages in Scripture that are universal favorites. When we turn to these we find that there are at least three qualities that seem to give them their value.

There is, first of all, the literary form. One who appreciates literary worth can not fail to be charmed with the rhythm and beauty of "Bless the Lord, O my soul, and all that is within me, bless his holy name." Or, "The heavens declare the glory of God, and the firmament showeth his handiwork."

The great texts that have come to be universally prized, however, contain something more than literary form. They possess some rich promise, or reveal some great principle of life, such as gives a deeper meaning to existence. No passage of Scripture is perhaps better known than John 3:16: "God so loved the world, that he gave his only begotten Son, that whosoever believeth on him should not perish, but have eternal life." There is no doubt about the significance of this verse being in the revelation that it gives of the character of God. If we turn to the Old Testament, where there is so much that does not seem to touch our modern life, we find occasional gems; as, *e. g.*, in the work of a minor prophet we read: "What doth the Lord require of thee, but to do justly, and to love kindness, and to walk humbly with thy God?" (Mic. 6:8). In what better way could a brief statement or ideal for life be presented? In the approach to the Scriptures that which we find of real value to ourselves is what endears a passage to us, and only as we appreciate its truth can we hope to make it real to others, for preaching is the expression of truth through the human personality, and that which has not become a part of us can not be imparted to others.

There are some texts whose significance is appreciated most, however, when used on special occasions. There is no way in which a preacher can better show his good taste and judgment than in the selection of suitable texts for the many unusual services in which he is called upon to participate or to conduct. To know how to use the great texts at such times is a splendid achievement. These unusual circumstances frequently invite the use of a passage in an accommodated sense. When so used the preacher takes the words out of their setting and accommodates them to the occasion. For example, a sermon was preached recently on John 18:12: "They seized Jesus, and bound him." After showing the connection in which the words were used, the text was applied to modern Christians, showing how by wrong habits of life Christian people prevented Jesus from expressing Himself through their personalities. If well used, an accommodated text can sometimes be made very striking and effective.

So we see that really great texts have their value because they are beautifully expressed, contain vital truth, and are suited to the occasion on which they are used. How can we discover such passages?

There can be no better answer than to say that they are to be found in one's own reading, but there must be in addition observation and an enriched experience. The reading without the experience would make the sermon material purely theoretical; the experience alone lacks its highest interpretation until related to eternal truth. It must always be, therefore, that as the preacher reads the Bible, and discovers its inner meaning and significance, he will know for himself the great texts. They never can be selected for him by others, for the experiences of men differ as do their features, and one would simply be accepting the reaction of another to divine truth, and not his own. Some seek help and may find suggestions in such books as dictionaries of great texts, but to depend upon such sources is an artificial way of selecting texts, and will never give a man the joy that he gets when he discovers them for himself. There are great passages in the Bible in abundance, and "they that seek shall find," but there is no other way.

QUESTIONS ON CHAPTER IV.

1. To what extent would you justify the use of the pulpit for a discussion of subjects other than those specifically religious?

2. Is there any incompatibility between topical sermons and the use of texts?

3. To what extent can the Scriptures be quoted as an authority to-day?

4. What seems to you to be the most valid reason for using texts in preaching?

5. Can you suggest any occasion when it seems best to omit using a text?

6. When would you recommend the use of more than one text for a sermon, and when only one?

7. Select six favorite passages of Scripture, examine them, and indicate the reason for the value placed upon them.

8. Can you suggest any method of Bible study or reading that will reveal the great texts of Scripture?

9. Would you justify the use of a highly emotional text?

CHAPTER V.

THE INTRODUCTION

IN dealing with the essential parts of a sermon we grouped under the heading of "Introduction" all the material that precedes the main divisions or the discussion of the theme. At the same time we may recognize the technical parts that are involved in this portion of the discourse, and if we are to go into details in approaching the introduction, perhaps the clearest way of doing it will be by following out the process through these steps.

Before considering the method of preparing the introduction, however, we will direct our attention to the purpose of it, for this will in some degree determine our method. There are three ends to be sought in this part of a discourse. The first of these is to *attract attention*. It is easier to gain attention at the beginning than it is in any part of the sermon. Psychologically, this must be true, for the mind has not yet become absorbed in any kind of reverie, nor come under the spell of any disturbing influences. People come to church favorably disposed toward hearing the sermon, and the beginning of the message is the place to get the attention, if the interest of the congregation is to be maintained throughout. In its strictest sense, of course, the purpose of the introduction is to introduce the theme, and the first step in this direction must certainly be to get the attention of the people to what is going to be said.

Gaining attention depends in part on the personality of the speaker. When men of genius begin to preach, and the people are eager to hear them, there is no necessity for considering any special plans or methods. There is, however, one little device of gesture which is sometimes used at the beginning of a formal address, which some preachers are known to use quite effectively. When about to begin speaking they have a way of looking into the faces of their audience, calmly and deliberately, yet without staring. There is a moment when the people ask themselves, "When is he going to begin?" That is the psychological time to speak. The people are in the mood of expectancy.

Another end to be aimed at in the introduction is the *development of interest*. Having heard the theme or text announced, one may say to himself, "Well, that does not interest me very much; I made up my mind on that question a long time ago," and here is the place for the preacher to show, which he can if he has any original material, that he wishes to discuss some phase of it that is new. Or it may be that he announces that he is going to speak on some subject or text which has no particular appeal to the individual, and it now becomes the preacher's task to compel an interest. This may be done by showing the place of his subject in the Christian program, or by presenting some novel discussion of it that will make it interesting to people in spite of themselves. In so much of our preaching we have to overcome religious bias, or perhaps the inertia resulting from commonplace preaching, due to so many sermons having been given on the subject that have failed to stir or benefit people. The masses are still interested in the Bible; they can still be moved by its teachings, but only when they are presented in an original and vital way. This means to be able to present a message in such a way that people will say afterwards, "I never heard the subject discussed that way before." It is in the introduction that we state the originality of our treatment of the subject, and thus arouse curiosity as to what we are going to say. It is just here where the preacher gets his grip on the audience.

The last thing aimed at in the introduction is the matter of *creating the atmosphere*. For religious services this is usually accomplished by the hymns and Scripture readings, and very little effort is necessary on the part of the preacher. All that he needs to do is to give a touch to this general atmosphere to give it a specific mood. It may be of praise as he contemplates speaking of the heavens declaring the glory of God. It may be of hope as he speaks of "the home over there." Or his purpose may be to arouse them to a sense of sin, to stir the conscience, and call them to repentance. This specific mood can generally be gained by the special character of the hymns and the Scriptures that are chosen. Where one can thus attract attention, awaken interest, and place the people in a favorable state of mind for the development of the theme, he has employed a model introduction.

Now, I can imagine some one who has not had much experience in preaching, and who is looking for some guidance in regard to method, saying: "Suppose I begin to prepare a sermon. I have the text before me, or I have decided upon a subject, how shall I proceed?" Let us address ourselves to this problem and illustrate the point by some sermons based on the text and by others based upon the subject. We will keep in mind the three steps that we grouped under the one heading, and this may assist us by giving directness to the method of approach. These are explanation, introduction and proposition.

Let us take, first of all, the sermon based upon a text. We can generally find a starting-place by showing its setting or its relation to the context, sometimes called, in the process of sermonizing, the explanation. This may be done by showing the connection of the text with the book in which it is found; as, for example, "Fear God and keep his commandments, for this is the whole duty of man" (Eccl. 12:13). Here the writer has been soliloquizing upon life, reviewing the various forms of ambition that control human activity, and testing the final value of materialistic ideals. He finds them unsatisfying. Then, after expressing his dissatisfaction with earthly objectives as an end in life, he states what does meet the soul's need, and says: "Let us hear the conclusion of the whole matter. Fear God and keep his commandments, for this is the whole duty of man." Thus the significance of the text is seen in its connection with a book which aims to present a philosophy of life. Or, again, we might take the words recorded in John 20:31: "These are written that ye may believe that Jesus is the Christ, the Son of God; and that believing ye may have life in his name." Here the importance of the text is seen in its connection with the gospel, revealing as it does the author's purpose, and showing those facts which the author regards as sufficient to lead to faith in Christ. Another illustration might be given of Paul's words in

Phil. 4:4: "Rejoice in the Lord always; again I will say, Rejoice." The fact that these words form part of a letter written from a Roman prison by one who had but little in this life to cheer or comfort him, shows the power and influence of the Christian faith.

Or a text may be explained from its setting in the chapter. The words of Jesus, "The fields are white already unto harvest," would naturally call for a description of the circumstances under which the words were spoken, showing the contrast of the green fields of grain with the spiritual harvest with which they were compared. "What shall I do that I may inherit eternal life?" asked the rich young ruler of Jesus. This is a popular and striking text. A review of the circumstances would again make a very natural approach, pointing out that wealth, even with morality added to it—a rare combination—still left the man unsatisfied regarding the welfare of his soul. Or, limiting it still further, a text may be explained without any purpose being served by relating it in any special way either to the book as a whole or to the chapter. Such texts are those in the Psalms, where very frequently the only connection with the context is the emotional attitude. Another example is the Proverbs, where a number of axioms are assembled without any vital connection or sequence. In Paul's epistles also many similar illustrations are to be found, especially at the end of the letters after he has finished the doctrinal section and is exhorting the readers. Many instances are also to be found in all parts of the Bible, where a verse can be taken out of its setting and treated independently of the context. Such passages usually appeal to us for their inherent truth, or because they express in rhythmic or striking form some sentiment that we desire to emphasize. In the case of such texts the approach would probably be a reference to the religious content of the passage, or our interpretation of it. Let us test a passage and see. In Ps. 84:11, and in the latter part of the verse, we read: "No good thing will the Lord withhold from them that walk uprightly." Now, how shall I begin? Well, I might ask myself, why did this text impress me? I reply: Because it contradicts the impression that the lives of those who serve God are a hard, sullen existence. This passage reminds me that it is a joyous, happy experience. The best blessings of Heaven are for God's people; we are better off than millionaire's children. This would form the first part of my introduction; in other words, that which impressed me in the text, and led me to select it, would probably be the point that I would emphasize in the introduction of a sermon.

Having finished now with the first step, that of explaining the text, we come now to the next point in working out our introduction. This really consists in relating the subject suggested by the text to the interests of the people as a whole. Now, suppose we continue the discussion of the passages we have used as illustrations. We have connected Eccl. 12:13 with the discussion of the book as a whole, in which it is found. We might now proceed to show that every individual has a philosophy of life, as is expressed by the things that interest him most, although he may not be disposed to dignify his mode of living with such an academic word as "philosophy." In other words, we go on to show the meaning in the text for our own lives. It is getting the sentiment of the text related to the thinking of the people, with the end in view of developing their interest in the theme. Take the next illustration, in John 20:31. Here is stated the purpose of revelation, and the sufficiency of the record to produce faith, through which alone there is salvation. This links up the problem of human destiny with our attitude toward Christ. Again it is indicating the significance of the Scripture for life. The passage in Philippians shows the power of faith in Christ to surmount all earthly difficulties—exactly the thing people are looking for in life. In all of these examples, and the same point can be shown with the other texts, the second step is a general discussion of the field of thought to which the text introduces us, and the interest is developed by showing the significance of the subject for people generally.

We now come to the third consideration in the working out of the introduction, which is the shaping of the proposition. Let us review again some of the passages we have been using for illustrations, taking an example from each group. We have noted in regard to Eccl. 12:13, first, the connection of the text with the book; next we have suggested how the truth of the passage has an interest for every individual; now we come, in the last place, to state our proposition, to indicate the specific objective which is to be the purpose of the sermon. Every sermon should have a proposition. It should nearly always be stated. There are only rare occasions, such as those when it would be unwise to reveal our conclusion on a subject, that this should be omitted. On these occasions by a succession of steps we seek an end for which we hope to win approval by the gradual unfolding of our thought. But even where no proposition is directly stated, there should always be clearly in the speaker's mind the definite point that he expects to make. This text in Ecclesiastes is one of those which can be turned into a good proposition. So the purpose might be stated this way: "To show that the fear of God and obedience to Him is the best ideal in life." The development of the sermon then would be to prove this to be true. Without a proposition the discussion leads nowhere, and though many interesting, and, perhaps, beautiful, things may be said, the message will fail to make any clear, definite or lasting impression upon the minds of the hearers. Let us now take an example from the second group, the words of Jesus: "The fields are white already unto harvest." In working out the introduction of this passage, we noticed first the explanation of the text in its setting in the chapter; next we would proceed to show the interest of the words to us, inasmuch as the words of Jesus are still true; then, in the third place, we state our proposition in definite terms, and say, "There is an urgent need for workers in the foreign mission field," or, "The text sets forth the appeal of the ministry as an avenue of service for young men," or, "An appeal to non-Christians is here given to enter the service of Christ." Any of these might be propositions based upon this text. If we take the passage in Ps. 84:11, we have noted, first, the reason that the text is significant in that it contradicts a popular conception of the meaning of the Christian life; next, we noticed that the passage has an appeal for all of us, because it points out the way to the enjoyment of that which we all seek; now we come to the place where we state the conclusion we expect to reach through our discussion, which might be, for example, "That the best things in life are the possession of God's people."

Before leaving the matter of the introduction, a word ought to be said about texts that are accommodated. When so used they are taken out of their setting and given an application entirely different from that which they had originally. While the same general principles still apply, a good plan in such cases is to refer to the fact that the text is going to be used in a sense different from that in which it is found in the Scriptures, and then explain the use that is going to be made of it. Very rarely, if ever, can an accommodated text be used without it being very desirable to explain the use which it is intended to make of it.

Let us next consider the method in constructing introductions to sermons based on a subject rather than a text. Such sermons should be unusual, yet it can be conceived how one might not have very clearly in mind any particular text, and yet be impressed with the need of speaking on some subject. Now, how shall he begin? The explanation of the text and its setting fail him here. Young preachers especially are given to preaching on subjects that cover a very wide field, probably for prudential considerations, so we will suppose that the subject of "prayer" has been selected. Another characteristic of young preachers, and of which every man ought to be cautioned, is to begin on such a subject by speaking of the lack of prayer, or on the negative aspect of whatever may be his topic, and then to lay the blame of modern indifference at the door of this neglect. This negative attitude rarely proves helpful. In preaching we need to be positive, to encourage, to

74

inspire faith, to quicken hope. Now, how are we to start on the subject of prayer in order to introduce it? The importance or significance of the topic often makes a good starting-point. Unless the subject has its origin in some current event or personal experience, this will often be the natural place to begin. To state it in another way, exactly the same procedure ought to be followed as has been suggested when a text is used, except that the first step—the explanation of the text —is omitted. The discourse is begun instead with some remarks which attract attention to the subject in a general way, and then the interest is developed by specifying the character of the discussion. The suggestion that was made earlier with reference to texts that are independent of the context might have value here also, that the particular thing about the topic that gives it special interest for the speaker may also prove a fitting way of introducing it to the con-gregation. Having aroused an interest in the subject in a general way, the next thing is to make a statement of the particular aspect of prayer that it is intended to stress. This may be to show: "The place of prayer in the life of Jesus," or "Prayer in the life of the early church as revealed in the book of Acts," or "The place of prayer in the life of Paul," or "Prayer is a necessity to successful church work," or whatever phase of the topic one proposes to discuss. So that the method of constructing an introduction is the same for a sermon based on a subject as for one that has its origin in a text, except that the first step is omitted and only the second and third applied.

When a preacher stands before his people week after week they soon become accustomed to his personality and general viewpoint of life. This makes it an increasingly harder task to attract and hold their attention unless he has been gradually gaining a greater hold upon their minds. A preacher is particularly in danger of losing attention at the beginning of his message by falling into the habit of always starting to speak by using the same form of words thus: "My text for this morning is taken from;" or, "My subject this evening is." Such forms, if they become a habit, are too commonplace, and remove all anticipation or feeling of expectancy, and so increase the difficulty of holding the attention. Nothing will help more to give freshness to the first part of the sermon than *variety* in form. Without being sensational at all, the first few sentences ought, as far as possible, to be surprises. There is no part of the sermon that gives greater scope for originality, and it can be done if one has a mind to work, and has anything of the orator's intuition.

While there are no substitutes or even suggestions that can take the place of the preacher's own resourcefulness in this matter, perhaps a few hints may help to point the way to success. A Presbyterian preacher, giving a sermon on prohibition, introduced it by telling an experience that he had but recently. He spoke of finding a man who was drunk. He described his pitiable condition. Many of the congregation were Scotch. He aroused feelings of mingled pity and disgust. Then he mentioned the thing that made the matter doubly sad. When he spoke to the drunken man he was answered back in a strong Scotch accent. Here was a very clever introduction. He told a personal experience, always interesting when not to glorify the speaker, and gained sympathy for his message right from the start. A local paper told of the discovery of an Indian's grave, in which were hat, moccasins, knife and fork, and a preacher used this current event as a starting-point for a sermon on the future life. Another, during a time when economic problems were disturbing the community, gave his congregation a message by contrast on "The Peace of Christ." The things that are uppermost in the public mind are always easy points of contact if they can be skillfully and tactfully used, but, after all, success in this matter depends upon the resourcefulness of the preacher. Let him remember that he must get the attention, and, having done that, to make a supreme effort to keep it.

Before closing this chapter it might be well to ask, "How long should the introduction take?" That depends on the length of the sermon. Since the sermon is the same as any formal discourse, except as the use of the text may determine the starting-point, the introduction to a sermon of twenty-five minutes should occupy the same time as an introduction to a twenty-five minutes' address on any other theme. It ought not to exceed five minutes, as a rule, just long enough to attract the attention, develop the necessary interest, and create a favorable atmosphere for the discussion of the theme. The time element, however, is not the important thing. It has a practical purpose, and not a theoretical or technical objective. If it takes twice as long to gain the desired end, then use it. Accomplish your purpose. Reach your goal. "Put it across." It is reported of Spurgeon that he would sometimes digress from his theme to tell a story or relate an anecdote to get the attention of an erstwhile indifferent person in his audience, or to get attention after some distraction, and he would be criticized for not sticking to his subject. Spurgeon, however, replied to the charge that he "stuck to his object" anyway.

When the object for which the introduction is used, has been accomplished, don't delay the discussion of the theme, however. Phelps, in his work on "The Theory of Preaching," likens the introduction of the sermon to the porch of a house. This illustration is very suggestive. We should not keep people too long on the porch when they are waiting to get into the house. It is neither good manners in the one case, nor good homiletics in the other.

QUESTIONS ON CHAPTER V.

1. Show that there are common elements in introductions to sermons based on the subject with those based upon the text.

2. How will the oratorical instinct help to give variety to the form of the introduction?

3. Is there any special reason why the first words of a sermon should attract attention?

4. Do you think that it is possible to interest people in every religious theme?

5. What general considerations would cause the length of introductions to vary?

CHAPTER VI.

THE MAIN DIVISIONS

THE main divisions with their development, or the discussion, as this part of the sermon is sometimes called, is the unfolding of the theme. What has gone before is only what the porch is to the house, so that from this fact the importance of the main divisions will be apparent at once. In making notes on a sermon it is evident that they have to be very much abbreviated, especially if they are to be used in the pulpit. They must be in the nature of an abridgment or synopsis of the whole sermon. This abridgment, or synopsis, when put in outline form, under concise headings, is what we term the main divisions.

Now, it may be asked, What is the real value of these divisions? Is it simply a formal consideration, or do the divisions serve a useful purpose? Let us examine the process of preparing a sermon. In beginning to work on any particular theme, the first thing one has to do is to collect the material. He may write down two or three headings under which these ideas are classified, as they are gathered, or may just write down at random the facts as they come to his mind, and leave the formal grouping of them till sufficient material has been brought together. Or it may be that he does some reading first of all on his subject, and just writes down the ideas that he thinks will be of value as he comes across them. Now he has assembled the material he expects to use. The next process is to classify and group it with reference to the working out of the proposition. Now, what has happened in this brief review of the process of sermonizing? It means that first of all it has been necessary to get the facts, then work them over in such a way as to group them logically, so that first of all divisions are an *aid to clear thinking.* More than that, the parts or divisions have been related to each other, which means that the whole discourse has been arranged in an orderly manner. In the next place, these parts have been related to the proposition, and thus the whole has been unified. So that clear thinking, orderly arrangement and the unifying of thought are the inevitable fruits of having the sermon constructed in this manner, and conversely, where this procedure is not followed, these fruits are lacking. It is not so much a question, after all, as to the value of having main divisions; the fact is, that where there is a definite proposition, with clear thinking and a logical arrangement of ideas, they are inevitable. It is a method that is not peculiar to the pulpit alone, but is common to all forms of public discourse where thought is properly organized, logically arranged and prepared for presentation to a popular audience.

Another great advantage in having the sermon material so grouped is that the *effort required by the preacher to remember his message* is thus *reduced to a minimum.* It would be a tremendous burden for him if he had to recall a number of detached ideas without being able to link them together by some kind of association. What usually happens in preaching when this arrangement is lacking is either that those who have a logical mind write down considerably and are more or less slaves to a manuscript, or else, if they speak without notes, there is no proper sequence of thought. Theoretically, of course, complete isolation of ideas is impossible, as all our mental activity is bound together by some kind of association. Nevertheless, relatively speaking, it is true that unless some logical arrangement has been given to one's ideas, his thought will be more or less rambling, incoherent and ineffective. On the other hand, where thought is properly organized, ideas follow one another in natural sequence as water flows down hill. When one's mental effort is thus reduced to a minimum, the power that would otherwise be necessary for recalling one's ideas is released for greater concentration on what is being said. This gives to the preacher greater freedom of expression, and both because he has thought his proposition through, and because of this released energy, his joy in preaching is greatly increased. He knows the road that he is traveling, he knows his destination, and also knows when he expects to reach it. Every preacher knows the difference of feeling he experiences before a congregation when he has complete mastery of his thought from those occasions when he has a kind of feeling that he has not made thorough preparation. The one experience is delightfully pleasant; of the other, we can neither use the adjective nor its modifier. Proportionately, as one has clearly and carefully worked out his main divisions, will he reduce his mental effort in the pulpit to a minimum and experience the satisfaction that grows out of complete mastery of his subject.

One other advantage, and the all-important one, still remains to be noted. The aim of preaching is to convince and convict the hearer. It is to be with a view to persuasion. Now, our minds are rational, and a clear and simple presentation of ideas always gives both pleasure and profit. We all delight in a well-arranged, orderly development of a theme, especially when it is one in which we have some special interest. Now, when we have organized thought for ourselves before we preach, we have done the same thing for the people who hear us. Sometimes we listen to an able speaker on some subject that has been for us a matter of great perplexity, and in an hour, or perhaps less, our ideas on the subject have taken definite form; or, in other words, the speaker has done for us in one hour what perhaps we have failed to do for ourselves in years. The conclusion reached has become our immediate conviction, but we usually want to remember the processes of the argument whereby the result was brought about. What is the most effective thing the speaker can do to make this possible? Is it not to group the thought under easily remembered headings, which are the divisions or steps in the argument? The main divisions, when remembered, should enable the hearer to recall the material as well as the development of the whole discourse. When well stated and arranged, they not only increase the preacher's joy and power, but also *give pleasure and permanent profit to the hearers.* We here give an illustration to show how this is true. Let us take the theme, ''Enduring Happiness,'' which might have for its proposition, ''Enduring happiness is only found in Christ.'' We suggest the following:

1. All seek happiness.

2. Every earthly expedient is transitory in character.

3. Happiness found in Christ is as enduring as life itself.

It is comparatively easy to develop these points, and the material of the whole sermon could be easily remembered by simply recalling these statements.

A question of some interest at this point is, "Should the divisions of a sermon be clearly stated each time one preaches?" Now, there are occasions when a formal statement would not be desirable. In a message where an appeal is made to the emotions more than to the intellect, anything that looks like calling attention to a reasoning process might weaken the effect, but even in such a case, in order that what is said may have permanent value for the hearers, the divisions ought to be impressed almost as forcibly as if definitely stated. There are not many addresses or sermons, however, of such a character that the line of thought can not be mentioned quite definitely. Very frequently it is desirable also, when beginning a new division of a discourse, to link it up with the preceding one, so that the progressive nature of the discussion may be apparent. In all sermons of a doctrinal or argumentative kind, as well as most others, the impression will be made more effective by clearly indicating the steps in the development of the thought. It will also add to the hearer's delight and make it easier for him to remember what has been said.

For one who is just beginning to preach, and for many others who have not had a systematic course in homiletics, the question will naturally arise at this point: "How am I to proceed in constructing the main divisions of a sermon?" This is an important question, and is one that is not without difficulty even for those who have done considerable work in English composition. Shall we, after deciding upon a theme, begin by making the outline, or should the material be gathered first, and the outline formed afterwards? Theoretically, of course, there could be no construction of an outline upon a subject concerning which nothing is known. In actual practice, however, we rarely, if ever, select a theme upon which our mind is a blank, but usually because an interest has been aroused either by the reading of a text, or by some experience that has stirred us. The subject is known or unknown to us only in a relative sense. So that when it comes to answering the above question, it may be said that both methods are adopted. Sometimes, when we have a sufficient knowledge of the subject to be developed, we may begin by making an outline, and then select the material to expand our ideas. This method is open to criticism as being in some measure unscientific, but the justification for it is that it will to a large extent give point and purpose to our reading or research work. Most preachers have settled convictions on the matters they present in the pulpit anyway, so that the working out of a theme is done by selecting facts rather than collecting them. The convictions behind the facts give force to the delivery.

The other method of collecting material or the facts before any attempt is made to construct an outline is the more scientific, for a right approach to a discussion on any topic is to bring together the facts, then classify and organize them afterwards. This would undoubtedly be the correct process to begin on any study about which one felt that he had very little information. This plan is usually the one that is suggested as the correct method of procedure by the writers on homiletics.

Probably most men use both methods, according as they have little or much knowledge on the theme it is proposed to develop. When a provisional outline is constructed at the beginning of the investigation, the mind should always be prepared for the introduction of new and unexpected material. This may possibly not only modify the outline, but also the proposition, and lead to a change of emphasis. Thus an outline made at the beginning should not be regarded as a mold into which all thought must be compressed, but rather as a tentative or suggestive way of organizing the material, which outline must be so plastic in its nature that it can ultimately be adjusted to whatever new facts are discovered in our research.

Suppose now, that the theme has been decided, the proposition stated and the material collected, what principles are to govern the arranging and stating of these divisions? Well, in the first place, they *must be related to the theme,* and have a direct bearing on the unfolding or demonstrating of the proposition. Just as, in literature, every sentence must contribute to the idea expressed in the paragraph, and every paragraph be relevant to the discussion of the chapter, and every chapter must be related to the book as a whole, so each main division of a sermon should form one step in establishing the truth of the proposition. If this quality is lacking from the constituent parts of the sermon, then the materials must either be irrelevant or are inadequately stated in the headings.

In the next place, they must have a *logical development,* or show progression of thought. As every sermon should have a beginning, a middle and an end, so there should be a moving forward, advancement in each part. The first division should begin the discussion and continue it to a place where the particular phase of the theme it is intended to cover is reached. Where the first ends the second should logically begin and carry onward the thought without repeating what was discussed in the first part. When there is material that could as well be placed under one head as under another, the sermon lacks proper arrangement, for any specific fact has one place, and one place only, in the development of a theme. So each division should lead the thought nearer to the point aimed at as the goal of the sermon; or, in other words, nearer to the demonstration of the truth of the proposition.

It will be observed in textual sermons, where parts of the text form the main divisions, that the progression of thought is not necessarily in the same order as it occurs in the passage of Scripture. An illustration of this point is given in one of Spurgeon's sermons, with the title, "As and So," which is based upon Col. 2:6. The text reads: "As therefore ye received Christ Jesus the Lord, so walk in him." The divisions as Spurgeon used them are:

1. The fact stated. "Ye received Christ Jesus the Lord."

2. The counsel given. "So walk in him."

3. The model presented. "As ye received him."

Here it will be noticed that the first part of the text is made the emphasis for the last part of the sermon. Why? Because the aim of the sermon determines the order of the material. It is working up to a point which constituted an appeal to the Colossians to maintain the enthusiasm with which they accepted Christ as a model for daily living. So the logical plan, which would be to use the parts of the text in the order in which they occur, making division three come first, gives place to the psychological. This method, however, does not conflict with the principle we have stated. It is an instance, if the paradox may be allowed, of the psychological method becoming the logical. Thus the logical way of reaching the climax psychologically, is to use the part of the text last that makes the most direct emotional appeal.

The same outline of C. H. Spurgeon's may be used to illustrate a third important quality of all good divisions. They should be *stated as simply as possible*. Thus in the above outline he says: "The fact stated, the counsel given, the model presented." Simplicity in style is always a virtue in rhetoric, and in no form of literature or speech is it of greater value or importance than in the construction of an outline. Sometimes only one or two words are necessary to hold in mind the thought. For example, a textual sermon on the theme of "The Risen Life" has been suggested in Col. 3:1, 2, as follows:

1. A challenge. "*If* then ye were raised together with Christ."

2. A command. "*Seek* the things that are above, where Christ is."

3. A contrast. "*Not* on the things that are upon the earth."

Simplicity, however, does not limit the headings to one or two words. Sometimes they may be made up of fairly long sentences, for this is often necessary to clearness. Inferential sermons, where the main divisions consist of a series of inferences taken from a text, are almost necessarily of this character. In one of Maclaren's sermons based upon Jas. 2:23, "He was called the friend of God," five inferences or divisions are given, and these are presented in five sentences. They are as follows:

1. Friends trust and love one another.

2. Friends have frank, familiar intercourse with one another.

3. Friends delight to meet one another's wishes.

4. Friends give gifts to one another.

5. Friends stand up for one another.

Each of these is a fairly long statement, but each is simple, and necessary for that kind of development. It ought to be noted, however, that the same balancing of form or diction should be carried out as far as possible within the limits of each sermon; that is, one division should not consist of just one word, and the next be a whole sentence. In actual practice there will not be irregularity of form, unless one does not have his starting-point or proposition clearly in mind. In technical terms, it usually results from not having a properly established *"fundamentum divisionis,"* or basis of division, as it is called in the terms of logic. When there is this uniformity, or balancing of phraseology, grace and beauty are added to the charm of simplicity. This adds elegance of style to the attractiveness of the presentation, and not only brings temporary delight to the hearers, but also helps to give permanency to the impression.

A fourth quality making for good divisions of a sermon is that the divisions should *complete the proposi-*

tion. We have noted that there should be a *terminus a quo* and a *terminus ad quem;* that there is a logical place to begin and a definite place to stop. The first division should begin the discussion and carry it as far as necessary to cover the ground designated by the heading, the second division should take it up exactly where the first leaves it, and so on through the succeeding divisions, and when the last is finished it should be clear to the mind of the preacher that he has completely established the proposition.

The process, after all, is very simple, and yet the marvel of it all is that so many educated men, preaching sermons continually, seem to fail sadly in applying these elementary principles. It seems remarkable, in view of the importance of preaching and the opportunity that the pulpit offers, that there should be so few men who have any adequate appreciation of the fundamental characteristics of effective sermons. The Scriptures are still as rich in treasure as they ever have been; there are resources in our daily experience as great as in days gone by, but these go to waste until we learn how to use them.

The question may naturally be asked at this point, "How many divisions should there be to a sermon?" The old idea was that there should be just three and no more. Such a plan, however, is purely arbitrary, formal and artificial. In putting together outlines it will often happen that there will be three divisions, but not because these were determined upon beforehand as the required number, but because they complete the proposition and therefore make any more unnecessary. Practically there may be any number from two to six. Obviously there could not be less than two, because if there were only one, then the statement of the one would become the theme or proposition, and the subdivisions, in turn, would become the main divisions. On the other hand, within the limits of a twenty-five minutes' sermon, only a limited number of positions could be enlarged upon or elaborated, and to increase this number beyond about five or six would simply be an enumeration of points, and not an elaboration of them. Usually there will be three or four main headings to each sermon, but this is decided in all cases by the proposition, the completion of which always determines the number to be employed.

A few suggestions might here be given as to certain general types of sermons, and the working out of divisions in regard to them. There is, first of all, a class of sermons which only calls for two divisions. These are based on those Scriptures where contrasts are presented. Illustrations are to be seen in such passages as the latter part of 2 Cor. 4:18: "The things which are seen are temporal; but the things which are not seen are eternal." There are also such Scriptures as the broad way and the narrow way; the house built upon the rock and the house built upon the sand. F. W. Robertson has an interesting sermon of this type, which is not only a good specimen of a sermon with two divisions, but is also attractive because of the method of development.

A noted writer on homiletics recommends four "constants": a constant cultivation of a more vivid sense of the realities of the gospel message; a constant cultivation of the homiletic habit; a constant cultivation of familiarity with source materials; a constant presence of a lofty standard of sermonizing.

THE PHARISEE AND THE PUBLICAN.

(Luke 18: 9-14.)

Introduction.—Sermon is a study in types, showing the danger of self-satisfaction and the value of humility.

I. SPIRIT OF SELF-SATISFACTION.

1. Satisfaction with negative goodness. He enumerated the faults he did not have. Verse 11.
2. Satisfaction with ceremonial acts. "I fast twice a week." Verse 12.
3. Satisfaction with himself caused contempt for others. "Even as this publican." Verse 11.
4. Satisfaction that led to cant. "God, I thank thee that I am not as other men." Verse 11.
5. Satisfaction led to fluency in prayer. It was preaching to God, and not praying.

II. SPIRIT OF PENITENCE.

1. Sense of guilt. "Me a *sinner.*"
2. Plea for mercy. "God be *merciful* to me."
3. Confession. "*To me* a sinner."

Conclusion.—Which is your model? Will you follow it now?

The approach to the outline here is very simple. As soon as a decision is made to preach upon such a theme, there is no difficulty about the divisions, as they are already determined. The skill in such a sermon will be seen in one's ability to suggest modern types corresponding to the Pharisee and the publican, and to make the application by such inferences as to arouse the spirit of self-examination on the part of the hearers. To do this well is a task of extreme delicacy, and requires unusual talent for its successful accomplishment.

To those who are just beginning to preach, or others who have difficulty in constructing outlines, there is a suggestion in regard to sermons based on narratives that may be of value. Just as certain Scriptures, where contrasts are involved, naturally lend themselves to sermons with only two divisions, so there are narrative sections that just as readily divide themselves into three parts. It will be understood, of course, that the suggestion here given is not intended to indicate that all these portions of Scripture should have exactly three divisions, no more or no less, as is the case with contrasts, but that, for those needing help, a three-part sermon can always be produced. Every narrative taken from the Bible, and this will apply particularly to the Gospels and the book of Acts, has three divisions: The *occasion*, the *event* and the *sequence*. These are very general terms, and may be modified by the individual narrative under consideration, but these three divisions of the narrative are always possible. The nature of the modification may be seen from an example. Let us take the account of the rich young ruler as it is given in Mark 10:17-31. These three parts may be divided into: 1. The meeting. 2. The conversation. 3. The outcome. If it is desired, these could be expanded to suggest more directly the character of each part as follows:

1. The happy meeting.
2. The interesting conversation.
3. The sorrowful outcome.

Another illustration might be given from the book of Acts (chapter 16), where we have the account of Paul's imprisonment and release. In this case the occasion, events and outcome might be transposed into arrest, imprisonment and release. Or, if it is desired to expand them still further, they might be stated as follows:

1. The unlawful arrest.
2. The cruel imprisonment.
3. The happy release.

The character of the modification will depend, of course, on the proposition, and the particular emphasis one desires to give to the narrative. Examples might be continued almost indefinitely.

This plan simply means that you take the account given from the beginning to the end, and cut it off in convenient sections for grouping the material. In using this plan, one could avoid giving the outlines the appearance of sameness by modifying each through reference to incidents peculiar to each narrative.

There is still further development of the outline possible, however, that deals with the content of each section. This consists in making the headings of the sermon not only recall the nature of the matter discussed in it, but also to indicate the preacher's attitude toward what is said in it. The ability to do this well is a mark of genius. This is one of the striking features of Maclaren's sermons. Here is an illustration. He has a sermon entitled, "The Name Above Every Name," based upon Acts 2:36. The text reads: "Let all the house of Israel therefore know assuredly that God hath made him both Lord and Christ, this Jesus whom ye crucified." The text is dealt with in such a way as to bring out the significance of the words "Jesus," "Lord," "Christ," and the three parts of the sermon are based upon these three names. Now, one way to state these divisions would be:

1. Significance of "Jesus."
2. Meaning of "Lord."
3. Expressiveness of "Christ."

Such a statement of the divisions, however, gives no clue as to what the preacher is going to say in the discussion of each of these, except that they will be defined. But note Maclaren's divisions:

1. The name "Jesus" is the name of a man, and tells us of a brother.
2. "Christ" is the name of an office, and brings us to a redeemer.
3. "Lord" is the name of dignity, and brings before us the king.

In these statements the significance of the words are brought out as part of the divisions. Notice also the splendid balancing of the sentences. There may be times when one might see an advantage in withholding his point to create suspense, or when a statement of one's position is best concealed for other reasons, but, apart from these considerations, the application of this method would be a great advantage. Let us examine the cases cited above, and apply this method. In the case of the rich young ruler, the outline suggested was: the meeting, the conversation, the outcome. These terms simply divide the narrative, but give no indications of the material involved. Now, to include the discussion, we modify them by saying:

1. The question asked Jesus by the ruler.
2. The conversation on eternal life.

3. The ruler's unwillingness to meet Jesus' requirements.

The first of these divisions tells who were brought together, and what brought them together, the second what the conversation was about, and the third what the sequence was. Thus the whole story is epitomized in the divisions.

The three-part sermons that we have been discussing so far, however, are those of the inductive type, where a narrative or considerable portion of Scripture is made the basis of a sermon. There is also the other type, where a sermon is built up on one verse, or, perhaps, even a part of a verse, from the Bible. A suggestion to help in this class of sermon is also given in the textual method. An illustration of this type is given in an earlier chapter under the title of "As and So" (see p. 84), where parts of the text itself are made the basis of the divisions. There are a great many texts that can be used in this way. Here is an illustration. In Ps. 34:5 we read: "They looked to him and were radiant; and their faces shall never be confounded." Here is a sermon on "The Radiant Life." The three divisions are suggested at once.

1. The origin of the radiant life. "They looked to him."

2. The influence on the beholder. "They were radiant."

3. The reaction before the world. "Their faces shall never be confounded."

Now, there are many kinds of sermons that are not included in the above types, and there is no way of describing how each and every kind of text can be approached, so that the divisions will be apparent.

The above only serve to give some definite help to those who are just beginning, or others who may be having some difficulties in their work, but the mastery of these should be a great help in all homiletical efforts.

From the contents of this chapter it will be seen that the writer has profound faith in preaching sermons that interpret and explain the Scriptures. This has become almost a lost art. The Bible, however, is as interesting as ever. It is the only book that is never off the press. In human interest Shakespeare and Milton are not in the same class. Those who think that the people are not interested in hearing the Scriptures explained certainly misunderstand the longings of the human heart. They want it, though presented in a fresh, original, helpful way. The only hope for our civilization is a deeper knowledge of the sacred writings and an application of their teachings to life, and the more Scripture there is taught and explained the better will the pulpit perform its function.

QUESTIONS ON CHAPTER VI.

1. Can there be clear thinking on a theme without clearly stated divisions?

2. What additional pleasure does a preacher get from having clear divisions to his sermon?

3. Why are the parables of Jesus easy to recall? Illustrate your answer.

4. What connection is there between the principle involved in the parables and in good sermon divisions?

5. Should all sermons have a logical development?

6. Illustrate by an original outline the difference between the logical and the psychological development of a sermon.

7. Illustrate by an original or selected sermon an outline possessing all the qualities referred to as necessary to make a good outline.

8. Would you regard eight divisions to a sermon too many. If so, why?

9. Give an original outline on some New Testament narrative, where only two main divisions are necessary.

10. What value would you attach to outlines of sermons given in magazines? What are the dangers from using them?

CHAPTER VII.

THE DEVELOPMENT

A S has already been suggested, there are two types of mind, each with its advantages and disadvantages. The one has ability to generalize and synthesize, but experiences difficulty in elaborating and explaining; while the other can amplify and enlarge without any very great effort, but has trouble in organizing thought. This being the case, some will have disadvantages above others in this part of sermon construction, although practice should to a large extent enable one to overcome this natural handicap.

There are several things necessary for the successful development of any sermon. In the first place, the material to be used must be well in hand. One may draw up an outline before intensively studying his theme, but he can not develop it well till he has mastered his facts. Without this, progress is impossible. Mere thinking will not produce a single fact unless it be the fact of our mental deficiency.

Sometimes it will happen, even after having read extensively, that one's mind may almost appear a blank. Generally, such a state of mind is due to lack of concentration, which, in turn, may be the result either of wrong physical conditions or from a conflict of the emotions which prevents relevant thought from reaching the focus of consciousness.

One can not do his best work unless his general health is good. Even when one is healthy, it is well to select the best time of the day for study, or, at least, to avoid trying to do important work when the mind is fatigued. There are very few who can do their best work in the afternoon. Some few can study well in the evening, while, to most, the hours of nine to twelve in the morning are the best, especially if one can be free from interruptions.

A disturbed emotional state always makes concentration difficult. A preacher with a family, who was having a financial struggle, found it so affecting his work that he said to the writer recently: "I simply can't study." Then, there is also danger from the more pleasant side of our nature, that which we call reverie or day-dreaming. A study of the habits of great preachers indicates that they were men of unusual concentration, and our work will improve in quality as we develop the habit of involuntary attention, or complete control of our mental life. Listen to the apostle Paul in this connection: "Whatsoever things are true, whatsoever things are honorable, whatsoever things are just, whatsoever things are pure, whatsoever things are lovely, whatsoever things are of good report, if there be any virtue, and if there be any praise, think on these things" (Phil. 4:8). In other words, strive after the control of your mind, become master of yourself, mentally as well as spiritually.

It is well for us to keep in mind also the fact that meditation is necessary for sermon development, even after these conditions have been met. One may spend much time thinking over his subject-matter and not appear to accomplish very much. Sometimes the mind seems very inactive, and, even in calling up some fact of past experience, one may find his memory quite irresponsive. Now, for the development of thought, the time element must be taken into consideration. How often have we tried to recall a person's name or address and given up in despair, only to awaken perhaps in the middle of the night, to have it presented to us like a flash. Evidently the subliminal or subconscious part of the mind continued the searching process after we had given up. This work of the subconscious part of our mental equipment is an important fact to be noted in the development of sermons. It is best to decide upon our theme for the Sunday as early in the week as possible, and give our ideas an opportunity to grow, or to relate themselves to those facts in the subconscious mind that we can use when we begin the actual work of committing our thoughts to paper. If one decides upon the theme and proposition, and develops it at one sitting, he is likely either to be very commonplace or else to say things that would have been eliminated or modified after thinking them over or meditating upon them.

Most preachers, after a sermon is over, have a kind of intuition regarding its general effect upon the congregation. Sometimes there is that depressing feeling of failure, which practically every alert preacher has experienced at some time or other. This ineffectiveness may be due to the materials, the delivery or the atmosphere. The last of these can not always be controlled, and may influence the delivery. The materials of the sermon, however, can always be of such a character as to prevent failure under the worst conditions, and under favorable circumstances can contrib-

ute much to success. The consciousness that one has
something important and interesting to say will enable
him to face a congregation with a feeling of confidence,
and give him pleasure in the anticipation of its delivery.
Now, what principles can be suggested for guiding
one in the selection of his materials? It is here where
judgment is most strikingly manifested, and where the
discriminating faculty has its best expression.

The first thing to be noticed is that it must be *vital*,
must have reference to the life of the people. In
reading one may discover many things in the realm
of scholarship, which, because of temperament, training
or experience, are interesting to him, but the important
thing in sermonizing is, How closely are they related to
the lives of the people who are to be addressed? Now,
there are various kinds of preachers. There are good
men without scholarship, and scholarly men without
much goodness, and then there are those of the best
class who have both of these qualities. Sometimes of
the first type there is the transcendental preacher, who
lives in the clouds, and talks about divine things as
though he were talking about a foreign country. He
is charmed with the delights of the unseen, and loves
the mystical, and people look on and say that he is
a good man, and he may be, but he has failed to
understand the great, throbbing heart of humanity.
His sermons are not related to the every-day life of
his community. Then, there is the preacher who is pre-
eminently a scholar. He lives in his library. He
loves books. Intellectual interests are his chief concern.
His sermons are interesting biographical sketches, re-
views of books or philosophical discussions; they are
full of classical quotations and references, and there are

sidelights on literary subjects, but with all this scholarship there is a lack of appeal because he does not
bring his thinking into the realm where the people live.

Now, there is no incompatibility in being a good
man or a scholarly man, and being alive to the religious
needs of the people. Goodness may demand respect,
and scholarship may awaken admiration, but a preacher's function in the community is not merely to be re-
spected or admired, but to help people so that his
hearers will be able to apply the teachings of Jesus to
all of life's activities. In order to do this, his messages
must have a contact with life. Only as they are of
this character can he hope to awaken and keep alive a
Christian interpretation of human existence and realize
his best in the pulpit.

In the next place, the material must be *relevant*
to the theme. This is particularly true of illustrations.
The mere fact that a story has a religious value does
not justify its use in a sermon unless it has a direct
bearing on the point being discussed. The one thing
that will help more than any other in "sticking to the
point" is a clear aim. If one sees the end from the
beginning, he will go straight to it, and will not be likely
to stray off into by-paths. But if he lacks a definite
aim, he is likely to be interested in a number of things
by the way, and may even give his congregation the
feeling that he is lost altogether. It ought not to
be very difficult for any man with a trained mind to
discriminate between the things that are pertinent and
to the point and those that are extraneous and out
of place, provided only he has a definite objective and
is industrious. It is possible for a minister to allow
the many details of his pastoral work to crowd out

the time that he ought to give to study, and, because he has failed to gather enough facts, to incorporate less relevant material in his sermon, or perhaps that which is entirely irrelevant. Such a man runs the risk of losing his powers of discrimination, and is thereby discounting his efficiency as a preacher of the gospel, and also his leadership in any part that he may have in civic affairs.

Having decided now that the material should be vital and relevant, a further quality to be sought after is *originality*. Even though the material is good and in keeping with the theme, one does not want to say the same thing that everybody else says, nor to say it in the same way. To do so makes one's preaching prosy, monotonous and uninteresting. To be original one must either say something new or say something old in a new way. How is this to be done, and how may one know when his sermon material is original? One way is to take some field about which many general statements are made, and, by collecting facts and data, show a conclusion that is based on scientific study. When this is done, results are often surprising. This is saying something new. Or one may take some old, familiar subject, and, by presenting it in a different way, cause people to say, "I never heard it discussed that way before." That is originality. One of the chief differences between the outstanding preachers and the rank and file, so far as the content of their sermons is concerned, is in this quality. Personality may be an important factor, but even this is modified with originality or lack of it in pulpit work.

Coming to the other part of our question, it is always possible to know, when developing a sermon, whether the ideas are original or not. All that one has to do is to ask himself, "Will this thought or the presentation of it be new to the congregation?" If it will, it is original and good; if it will not, it is more or less commonplace and uninteresting. One may know this as he develops his sermon, and he will know it more as he preaches. If he has the consciousness that it is new, it will thrill him as he speaks, and he will have the joy of seeing the faces of his congregation looking at him with intense interest as if some pleasing and helpful thought had come across their mental horizon.

Originality is, in a measure, inherited, being a part of our personality. It can be developed, however, just as personality can. I would suggest three ways in which this very desirable quality can be attained, and, unless one or more of these methods are applied in every sermon, it may be marked down for a certainty that it will be uninteresting, dull and ineffective.

The first of these to note is *intensive study*. What is more enjoyable or more desirable in a speaker than to hear him discuss his subject as if he knew all there was to know about it? We all know the effect of a sermon or address when some one says about the speaker, "He certainly seems to know his subject." The Great Preacher spoke as one having authority. There is nothing much more pleasing in a speaker than to hear it said of his message, "It was new to me." To apply this method to the regular work of the pulpit means that, if one has a knowledge of Hebrew or Greek, he will seek to find out the fine shade of meaning in the original, that he will compare parallel passages, con-

104

sult both the Authorized and the Revised Versions
as well as modern translations, and whatever outside
reading may be suggested by the theme. Many subjects are capable of statistical demonstration, such as
missions, Bible-school work and evangelism. To use
these figures, the making of graphs, and tabulating of
results on almost any phase of Christian work will
nearly always give some interesting results, and is
always original. Intensive study also means that all
a preacher's resources of knowledge and training will
be used in sermon preparation. The one who speaks
in platitudes and generalities alone is never original.
Just here is the special danger, the besetting sin, of
those whose natural gifts enable them to speak fluently
with little study beforehand. While they may seem
to "get by," that is not the final test; it is a question
of how much the people have been helped by their
public efforts. Probably the old Latin proverb which
says, "*Ex nihilo nihil fit*" (out of nothing, nothing
comes), is not without its application here, in the realm
of mind as well as matter. One who neglects to make
adequate preparation loses one of his three opportunities of becoming an original speaker.

Originality may also be attained by means of *ap-
propriate illustrations*. This method may be applied
not to one point only, but to a division, or even to a
whole sermon based on analogy. If it is apt, very often
more can be accomplished by this simple method than
by a prolonged exposition. Some of the great evangelists especially have used this plan with wonderful
skill and effect. The fact that the process is less profound than the preceding one is no reflection on the
method. The important thing is to enforce one's point

and to do it effectively, and whatever legitimate means will accomplish that object are both good and desirable. A lecturer on prohibition once came on to a public platform carrying what resembled a roll of carpet about a yard wide. It was made out of calico or some similar material, and on it were pasted newspaper clippings telling of accidents, assaults, murders and crimes of various kinds within a stated period that resulted from liquor. At the climax of his address he unfolded the roll, and then gave a classified summary of the crimes. This illustration immediately demonstrated the magnitude of the evil in such an original way that no one present would be likely to forget it. No one else had ever done that. Originality in illustration can often be shown by the use of maps or charts. This is a particularly forceful way of presenting statistical facts. People are always easier to interest when the speaker has a map, graph or chart to which he can refer. Pulpit formalities and conventionalities have probably kept us from doing many things along this line that would assist in making our preaching effective, and probably a reaction from this attitude is responsible for extreme methods being used in some modern pulpits. The truth, however, is along the *via media*. There is a wholesome use of story, anecdote, chart and graph, and we should take advantage of these so far as cultural standards and pulpit dignity will permit.

A third method of acquiring originality is by means of *unusual application*. Jesus once told His audience of a wealthy farmer who planned many years of happiness on the basis of material resources, but who died the same day that he completed his plans. He then said: "So is he that layeth up treasure for himself and is not rich toward God." In a certain college town in the middle West there was a moving-picture theater well known among the students by the name of "The Majestic." It was advertised in the street-cars of the city by the words, "Get the Majestic Habit." One of America's great preachers once appeared before the students at their assembly and announced as his theme, "The Majestic Habit." It immediately arrested attention, established a point of contact, and put the students in a friendly attitude. The speaker then proceeded to urge upon his hearers the habit of being majestic or princely in conduct. The application was so original that the message was easy to remember, and the preacher both succeeded in giving a splendid address and by his originality in gaining the good will and appreciation of his audience. When originality adds to dignified effectiveness, be original!

Any one who will study the effect of his addresses will find that those that interest, that grip, that win, have their success very largely in their originality. He will also observe that this quality is always secured by one or by a combination of the methods mentioned above. He can not be original without them; he can not fail to be original if he applies them. Can every man attain these qualities? Why not? By means of training and habits of observation, this ability to express oneself ought to be within the reach of all. Every man ought to make it his objective and work for it till he secures it. It is one element that is essential to success on every occasion, and without which no sermon can be very interesting or make a lasting impression.

Now, if one selects such material as is vital to the life of the people, that is relevant to his subject, and is original, only one thing further is necessary in the development, and that is the logical arrangement of it. Just as the main divisions should be the logical working out of the proposition, or as the chapters of a book should all bear a logical relation to the title, so now the development of each part of the sermon should be for the purpose of explaining, amplifying or illustrating the title or statement of each division. One may have many good ideas, but if they lack coherence and order, the development is unfinished. The material must be properly organized, given a logical relationship, and the thoughts made to succeed one another progressively. Up to this point they are like materials for a building, necessary for its construction, but the character of the building depends upon the arrangement of the materials. Nothing will be of greater service for this purpose than to keep clearly in mind the aim of the sermon, so that every part will be adapted with the right end in view. There is an abundance of sermon material all around us, but, like life itself, the standards we apply determine our selection. If the right principles control this process of discrimination, and we are looking for the best, there is no reason why a preacher should not have something helpful for every occasion, nor why he should not preach in an interesting and effective way.

We next come to a discussion of the various literary forms that may be employed in the development of sermons. There are at least four methods that may be used, and the ability to use these well will add greatly to one's efficiency. If the plan of development used by those who have become powerful in the pulpit be observed, it will be seen that all of them excel in one or more of these methods. A great advantage, growing out of an examination of one's ability to apply these methods, is, that he can select the plan that suits him best for any special occasion that may arise. The nature of the subject for those who do not have any decided preference will often determine the rhetorical method most desirable.

The first method to notice is the *descriptive,* or pictorial, way of preaching. People like pictures, and any man who has the power to take the narratives of the Scripture and present the scenes in pictorial form will always have a crowded and interested congregation. One may object that the method is elementary, but in justification it may be said that it works. Even educated people enjoy having the setting of Scripture narratives painted for them, because nearly every one has tried to image those scenes from childhood, and so is interested in having another complete his own inadequate images.

This art is one that can, in a measure, be acquired. If preachers who are underdeveloped in this regard would introduce a picture into each sermon, even though it may take but a minute or two of time, the faculty would soon be developed. To succeed in painting pictures for an audience one needs to meditate upon some scene, then close his eyes and visualize it, and then, after having seen the people, the place and the events as clearly as if on canvas, if he has a good use of language, he can describe for others what he has seen. He can not, however, hope to describe for others what he has not seen. This method of developing a sermon is one of the easiest, as well as one of the most effective, for those to whom it comes naturally because of a vivid or trained imagination; to others much time and effort are necessary in order to become even moderately proficient.

Another method of development is by the *story and anecdote*. This is very closely related to the preceding, inasmuch as description is often a part of a good story. Some preachers use this method to very great advantage, especially the great evangelists. They usually state the division, and then, after a few words of comment, proceed to illustrate it, leaving the story to establish the point. Every one loves a good story.

A good story has several outstanding characteristics. There is a beginning, and this is important, because it makes the contact. So in childhood stories we say "Once upon a time." In the Scriptures we read: "A certain man had two sons." Or attention may be gained by saying, "When I was in Africa." Then there must be action, or a succession of events, to carry the interest forward. Did you ever ask what made the story of the prodigal son so popular? Notice the action. The son packs up, leaves home, takes a journey, associates with the wrong company, loses his money, meditates, starts for home, meets his father, then there is a celebration. In the next place, a good story must have a climax. A funny story that is not funny is really one without a climax. Then there is the conclusion, and when a story is ended it should not be spoiled by comments. A study of the stories used by almost any of the successful preachers will reveal how prominent these qualities were in their illustrations, and will abundantly repay any aspiring evangelist. We can all remember apt stories that we have heard from preachers. Often the substance of a sermon could be repeated, and many would hardly be aware of the repetition, but let the preacher use the same stories that he gave before, and all who heard the sermon previously will recognize it immediately. If stories are so easily remembered, their value is apparent, especially when associated with some great principle of life.

A third rhetorical form of development is the *expository or explanatory* method. It consists in taking a passage of Scripture and giving an extended explanation or interpretation of it. Sometimes it may be used all through the sermon, or may be combined with any of the other methods. Very frequently it is employed at the beginning of the discourse only. It has its place there for two reasons. First of all, that is the logical place for it, because it is taken up with explaining the text which comes in the introduction. In addition to this, it is also a psychological place, as the appeal to the emotions and will ought to have a foundation in the intellect first. There is one danger with this otherwise very desirable method, and that is a commonplace, unoriginal and uninteresting development. In order to preach sermons of this type successfully, one must be able to think clearly and express himself forcibly. To possess the faculty of using this method well is a rare gift, and is undoubtedly the best of all. It makes a deeper impression, appeals to thinking people, and can be made popular.

A fourth method which is not a very common one, but which is sometimes practiced very effectively, is what might be called the *catechetical* method. I have designated it thus for lack of a better term. It is the principle of the catechism applied to public discourse. This consists in asking a series of questions which differ from rhetorical questions, in that an answer is given to them. The following may be cited as an example to illustrate the process. It is based upon Acts 10: 1-8. The questions only are stated. Who was Cornelius? What kind of a man was he? What happened to him? What did he see? What did he do? What was told him? Did he obey? It can easily be seen that all this could be given in narrative form in about one-half of the time, but, unless it were well done, it would probably only be about half as interesting. When this method is employed it should not be applied too formally. The questions themselves should be simple, vital and progressive. They should be simple, so that the point can be easily apprehended and readily grasped. They should be vital, so that they will arouse interest, and the audience be anxious to know the answer. They should be progressive, so that they will lead to some definite end which harmonizes with the objective of the sermon. It is a method particularly suitable for young people's services, and can sometimes be made quite impressive for audiences of older people also.

Nearly every preacher has some rhetorical power that will bring to him the fullest measure of success, and close examination will reveal the fact that it is in one or the other of the above-mentioned ways. The thing for each one to do is to discover himself and his powers, and use them; also his defects, and overcome them. If one finds that he is weak in descriptive ability, let him, as suggested, make a studied effort in each sermon to paint a picture; if he lacks in the use of illustrations, let him begin by using one occasionally, and note its effect. The thrill that we get in speaking, and the reaction from the audience, is the best way of estimating the value of our work. Jesus' words in another connection can well be applied as a motto here, "Watch and pray." Watch the audience and pray for the help that never fails when we do our best. With all the assistance that is available in modern times to aid preachers in their work, it seems a sin when educated men preach to indifferent congregations—and the sin is not always on the part of the congregation. It simply means that the preacher is not realizing his best for the greatest of all tasks committed to human beings—that of making known the glad news of the gospel of Christ.

It only remains now to notice the psychological approach to arranging sermon material. To do this we need to recognize the various phases of consciousness. In leading a person to the acceptance of any new viewpoint that we expect to be permanent, three stages are necessary. In the first place, there must be an appeal to the intellect. Truth must have a rational basis. The position should be stated and explained in such a way as to gain mental assent. Then the next step is to arouse feeling in order to produce the right emotional attitude toward the position presented. Just here is where the value of illustrations comes in. It is easier to stir the feelings by means of illustrations than in any other way, so that they have a place in the rightful development of a sermon. The last appeal is to the will, in order to lead to action, and the most natural way is by exhortation. So the apostle Paul says: "I beseech you therefore, brethren, by the mercies of God, to present your bodies a living sacrifice, holy, acceptable to God, which is your spiritual service."

Any proper development of a sermon or a series of sermons should take into consideration these three phases of consciousness. A sermon to the intellect alone rarely leads people to action, one to the feelings alone may lead to action, but on insufficient evidence, and when the emotion subsides, the decision no longer influences the life; while a rational appeal can not be made to the will—to change the conduct of life— until one has been shown that he is wrong, his emotions stirred, and his conscience aroused.

Questions on Chapter VII.

1. To what extent is a knowledge of the Bible helpful in developing a sermon?

2. Write an original description of some Bible scene.

3. Present a good story taken from an evangelistic sermon, and state the qualities that cause you to regard it so highly.

4. Can a sermon be interesting that lacks originality?

5. Is it easy for all preachers to use vital themes?

6. What kind of training should help a man most in the selection of relevant matter for sermons?

7. In using an extended portion of Scripture for a sermon, what help would one have in developing it?

8. What conditions are necessary in order to the best results from study?

9. What advantage is to be derived from continued meditation on one's sermon?

CHAPTER VIII.

THE CONCLUSION

THE main divisions and their development complete the proposition. Then, why a conclusion? It is that part of the sermon where the argument is reviewed or an appeal is made to apply the truth of the proposition. The strength or weakness of this appeal is determined in a large measure by the clearness with which the proposition has been set forth, and the effectiveness with which the sermon has been delivered. What it means to the preacher—in other words, his own conviction about it—will also have an important bearing on the forcefulness of the appeal. Let the preacher ask himself the question, as he prepares his conclusion: "Will this sermon convince the people of the truthfulness of the proposition if they do not believe it already and come with an open mind?" "Would it arouse or convince me if I were indifferent and heard it?" Unless he believes it himself, and believes it intensely, it can hardly be expected that he will convince others. If it be an appeal to better living, then there must be a serious effort on the part of the preacher to carry out that ideal in his own life. People usually interpret what a man says in the pulpit by what he is out of it. A doctrinal or argumentative sermon may be more or less successful without the element of character entering in to the same degree, although it is very desirable here; but to lead people to accept and apply higher moral and religious ideals requires the same ambition in the preacher. So, what a man is out of the pulpit greatly affects what he accomplishes in it. One should have a deep conviction regarding the proposition, and a feeling that it is vital to the life of the people, and then preach as if he expected them to accept the message. Nothing is more apparent in apostolic preaching than this fact, that when they preached they expected the people to believe in and accept Christ. Only as there is this conviction can there be a good conclusion, for it is incongruous to appeal to people to believe and apply that which we neither believe nor apply ourselves.

From the literary and rhetorical standpoint there should be careful preparation with the closing part of a sermon, because the importance of the last five minutes of a sermon is out of all proportion in effect to the time occupied. If one spends twenty minutes elaborating, demonstrating or illustrating a proposition, and does it well, and then has an ill-prepared five minutes' conclusion, people will leave with the feeling that it was just an ordinary sermon. On the other hand, suppose the substance of the first twenty minutes be poor in quality, and then let the last five minutes be very interesting, and people will go away and say it was a splendid sermon, that the preacher was not at all tiresome, and they will anticipate his next discourse with pleasure. A weak ending always leaves the congregation with an indifferent feeling, and the only way to prevent that effect is to remove the cause. No preacher can afford to be careless about this part of his sermon. Whatever one may feel regarding the remainder of the sermon, it is only courting failure to have an uninteresting, ineffective or unimpressive conclusion. This is all the more blameworthy because there are a few simple methods that can be applied which will save ourselves the discomfiture and the audience the disappointment.

Of the various methods used to make a conclusion convincing, we will notice, first of all, the device of *recapitulation*. As the etymology implies, this is carried out by restating the main divisions. If the divisions have been clearly stated and logically developed, the restatement of them will be an abbreviation, or digest, of the whole discourse. The proposition is the sermon condensed, and it will now be given in such a form that it can be comprehended, remembered and made a working hypothesis for life. This method brings before the congregation in a few sentences all that has been said, and so the mind, which has been able to see the development step by step, can now get a glimpse of the cumulative effect of the whole discussion.

Recapitulation, as a form of conclusion, is most fitting and most suitable in reasoned discourses where there is the logical working out of some doctrinal position or viewpoint of life. After presenting a number of arguments, it is the natural way of making the force of all of them together felt. In sermons of this type, it would generally be an advantage to state clearly the proposition and also the different steps in the development. For other kinds of discourses, however, where the method of recapitulation is adopted, it should be less formal and more rhetorical, being more in the nature of what Vinet calls a *resume,* or general review of the train of thought, rather than the formal steps in its unfolding. This method is a very simple one, and enables the speaker to throw all his force into the appeal of the proposition.

Another method for a good conclusion is the use of an *illustration.* This plan has several advantages, and perhaps is the simplest of all. If it be a story or an anecdote, it is easy to hold the attention, and so the preacher has the interest of the whole congregation at the place in his sermon when it is most to be desired. In the next place, the conclusion is the place where emotional heightening is required, and an illustration makes a more direct and effective appeal to the emotions than any other plan of presenting thought. Illustrations from family life and involving parental respect, as well as those that have a patriotic basis, are always impressive for finishing a discourse. Love of mother and love of country are the two appeals of which people never tire, and incidents that have their origin in either of these sources, if sincerity be manifested in the telling of them, always awaken a very responsive chord. In the last place, the conclusion is designed to lead to action, and appeals through illustrations, because of their emotional value, are the most powerful of all.

Another very effective way of finishing a sermon is the use of some *well-chosen and apt quotations.* Such quotations should, however, be from memory. To read from manuscript at the end of a sermon is always weak. Quotations from choice hymns and from literature, when apt, always make a pleasing finish to a message. When the quotation expresses the sentiment of the proposition, it is particularly strong. Many selections from the realm of literature have both emotional value and richness of language, and when, in addition, they express the sentiment of the message, they complete all the elements to be desired in a good conclusion.

Another method much used by great speakers and preachers is to write down the last three or four sentences of the discourse. One then not only knows where he is going to finish, but also how he is going to finish. It saves one from having to grope about for a good stopping-place. In his recent book on "The Art of Preaching," Dean Brown remarks: "I want to have the last four sentences definitely in mind so that I may not be left circling around in the air, like some helpless crow, flying to and fro above a rail fence where the stakes have all been sharpened, seeking in vain for some suitable place to light."

QUESTIONS ON CHAPTER VIII.

1. Why is it more important to prepare the conclusion than any other part of the sermon?

2. What should be the aim of the conclusion?

3. What is the psychological place for the sermon to end?

4. Prepare an outline with the conclusion written out in full.

CHAPTER IX.

TYPES OF SERMONS

SERMONS may be classified in a number of ways according to the purpose one has in view. This may be done, for example, according to the audience addressed, and so be grouped as sermons to Christians and sermons to non-Christians, or, again, under this same heading, as sermons to young and to adults. Or the basis may be made the occasion on which they were delivered, and the groups be ordinary or special occasions. As purpose is the controlling factor in classification, however, the basis that seems to be most useful is the *use made of the text*. This creates a difficulty in regard to sermons for which no text is used, as it is obvious that they would not come within the scope of this classification. Such sermons are, however, topical in character, and for practical purposes may be so recognized.

According to the basis suggested, sermons may be divided into four kinds—textual, topical, expository and inferential. We will review each of these in the order given.

1. *The Textual Sermon.* This kind is one in which the text is the theme, and the various parts of the text are used as the main divisions of the sermon. An illustration of this type of sermon is given below in the outline of C. H. Spurgeon's, to which reference has already

been made. In this it will be seen that the divisions of the sermon are based on parts of the text.

AS AND SO (Col. 2:6).

"As therefore ye received Christ Jesus the Lord, so walk in him."

Introduction.—Recollection of their experience in conversion is used as a basis of continued loyalty to Christ.

I. FACT STATED. "Ye received Christ Jesus the Lord."

1. Personality of one received. Christ Jesus, *the* Lord.
2. Threefold character in which received Him: Christ, Jesus, Lord.
3. Looking away from self in the act of receiving.
4. Certainty of the experience: Ye *have* received Him.

II. THE COUNSEL GIVEN. "So walk in him."
Walking suggests:

1. Life.
2. Continuance.
3. Activity.
4. Progress.

III. THE MODEL PRESENTED. "As ye received."
How was He received?

1. Gratefully.
2. Humbly.
3. Joyfully.
4. Effectually.
5. Unreservedly.

Conclusion.—Let us continue to manifest these qualities in our daily lives.

Sermons of this character are valuable because of the way they may be made to interpret the Scriptures. People still love to hear the Scriptures explained, and the man mighty in the Scriptures will not lack for a congregation to preach to if he is reasonably well endowed for his work in other ways. People love to hear familiar texts explained in such a way that truths overlooked in a cursory reading are brought to light. The method also has the charm of simplicity, and stimulates reading and study of the Bible.

2. *The Topical Sermon.* With this kind the text merely suggests the subject. Thus Heb. 11:1, which reads, "Now faith is the assurance of things hoped for, a conviction of things not seen," may be used on the topic of "Faith," but beyond suggesting the subject no further use is made of it. Any one of several other texts could just as well be used; for example, "Have faith in God." In a sermon of this type, the subject is usually the genesis of the discourse, and the text used is a secondary consideration. The following outline is a specimen of this class of sermon.

THE WONDERFUL JESUS (Isa. 9:6).

"His name shall be called Wonderful."

Introduction.—"Wonderful" is a fitting epithet to apply to Jesus. Every stage of his life was extraordinary. "I know men, and I will tell you that Jesus was not a man. Everything in Him amazes me. His spirit outreaches mine, and His will confounds me. Comparison is impossible between Him and any other being in the world. He is truly a being by Himself." —*Napoleon.*

He was wonderful in:

I. BIRTH. There are many things in life we can not understand. Jesus' birth is but one illustration. All things are possible with God.

II. MINISTRY.

1. Teachings. Jesus' teachings exceeded the authority of Moses. "Ye have heard," "but I say unto you." "I think Christ's system of morals and religion, as He left them with us, the best the world ever saw or is likely to see." —*Benjamin Franklin.*

2. Miracles. Miracles of Jesus are embodied in the heart of the gospel narratives, and to remove the supernatural element is to destroy the narrative. "I believe Jesus Christ to be the Son of God. The miracles which he wrought establish in my mind His personal authority, and render it proper for me to believe what He asserts."—*Daniel Webster.*

3. Sinlessness. The sinlessness of Jesus a miracle in the moral realm. Only one in Scriptures set forth as perfect man, and accepts that estimate of Himself. His character has challenged criticism for two thousand years.

"The sinlessness of Jesus is the crowning or root miracle which lends credibility to all others: a miracle unique and separating Him from all men, a miracle which convinces us that at this point at all events He has transcended all human experience and passed into a region beyond all human calculation."

"If ever man was God or God man, Jesus Christ was both."—*Byron.*

III. DEATH. Its wonderful character seen in:
    1. Agents. Pharisees—the religious people of His time.
    2. Circumstances. Selection of murderer instead of Christ.
    3. Way endured. Praying for enemies. So wonderful that the centurion said: "Truly this man is the Son of God."

IV. RESURRECTION. So wonderful the disciples could not comprehend it. Thomas said: "Except I shall see in his hands the print of the nails, and put my finger into the print of the nails, and put my hand into his side, I will not believe."

Conclusion.—Every phase of Jesus' life and work is wonderful. "Jesus is the incomparable man to whom the universal conscience has decreed the title 'Son of God,' and that with justice. Whatever may be the surprises of the future, Jesus will never be surpassed."—*Renan.*

The above is a good illustration of the strength and weakness of this type of sermon. It belongs to a class peculiar to young preachers. The natural fear with many young men is that they will not have enough material to make a sermon, and so a comprehensive subject is selected. So, topics like "prayer," "faith," and similar ones, are chosen, and, in making three or four heads under this general theme, the development becomes commonplace. Lack of originality is the outstanding weakness of topical sermons. The way to overcome this danger is to narrow the field, and give to the theme depth rather than breadth. What is on the surface nearly every one knows; what is below

124

they do not. "Faith," as a subject, may thus be limited to "Faith as an essential to progress," or "Triumphs of faith," which demands a more intensive development than is required by "Faith" without any limitation.

Another interesting feature of the topical sermon illustrated above is: The way in which a synthetical discourse of this kind, covering a wide field, may be made effective. Any one of the subdivisions might easily be made the basis of a sermon. To attempt to discuss them in detail would be an impossible task. Each is just mentioned, however, a few words said about it, and then a quotation is given from some recognized authority as an alternative for a discussion. In this way the sermon is complete and comprehensive, and the quotations are a good substitute for an otherwise necessary discussion. It will also be observed that the whole sermon is developed around the word "wonderful."

This is the easiest kind of sermon to prepare, and is, generally speaking, the least effective, because of the danger from lack of originality. It makes less use of the text than any kind, and when the subject covers a large field makes less demand on the preacher.

3. *The Expository Sermon.* The expository sermon is one in which the text is the theme, and the whole sermon is a discussion of it. The text may be half a verse of Scripture, a whole verse, several verses, or an entire chapter. To take a portion of Scripture and explain it, however, does not make an expository sermon. A sermon is a unit. There must be a proposition, a definite point to the discussion, and the explanations must all contribute to the elucidation of that

125

point. Below is given an exposition of the nineteenth Psalm, abbreviated as far as is possible consistently with good sense:

SOME ASPECTS OF RELIGION (Psalm 19).

Introduction.—Psalm of meditation.

  I. NATURAL RELIGION.

    "The heavens declare." They speak forth, make known. They preach.

    "Day unto day." Not twenty-minute sermons twice a week, but continually.

    "Showeth knowledge." Our sermons may not impart knowledge to hearers; heavenly preachers "show knowledge."

    "There is no speech nor language." They don't speak like human preachers, in one language, but universal language.

    "Their voice is not heard." Contrast again seen. They preach, teach and yet do not speak.

    "Their line is gone out." Line of harp or bow. Effect is "life unto life," or "death unto death."

  II. REVEALED RELIGION.

    "Law of the Lord is perfect." It is perfect for its purpose—to reveal God and show man the way of life.

    "Testimony of the Lord is sure." As reliable as perfect. He "is not man, that he should lie," nor is His word changeable as is academic knowledge.

    "Making wise the simple." Highest wisdom known to world is living in harmony with His will.

"Statutes of the Lord are right." Man's laws
are often imperfect, only reflecting the standards of the countries where they are made.
God's in harmony with His character.

"Rejoicing the heart." Doing God's will is secret
of joy in life.

III. PERSONAL RELIGION.

"Secret faults." Those which are beyond the
eye of man. Sins of thought.

"Presumptuous sins." Those based in passion.

"Great transgression." Separation from God.

Conclusion.—The meditation ends where all thought
of God should end, in a prayer that the life
may be better.

This Psalm is a complete thought on the subject of
religion, discussed from three viewpoints. Instead of
regarding the whole Psalm as one sermon, however,
any one of the three divisions might be used to make
an expository sermon. Thus verses 7-11 might be used
under the title, "Characteristics of God's Word."
Its development would show how it was perfect, sure
(verse 7), right, pure (verse 8), clean, true (verse
9), valuable, pleasant (verse 10), helpful (verse 11).
Expository sermons have the same value as textual in
that they are built upon the text of Scripture. How
much, after all, there is to explain even in these familiar passages! What congregation would not listen
with pleasure to any man who believed in the Bible
when he demonstrated the above passages?

4. *The Inferential Sermon.* In the case of the inferential sermon, the development consists in a series
of inferences drawn from the text. The following by
Alex. Maclaren will illustrate this point:

127

THE BETRAYAL OF JESUS (Matt. 26:50).

Introduction.—1. The text constitutes Christ's last appeal to Judas. 2. The text shows the limit to which God goes to win men, and the persistency with which men turn from Him.

I. PATIENCE OF CHRIST'S LOVE.

1. "Friend" is an expressive word—acquaintance, companionship.
2. Has a deeper meaning when used by the Son of God.
3. Love extended to Judas is not refused us by anything we can do.

II. PLEADING OF CHRIST'S LOVE.

1. Sin which does not turn away God's love does modify it. (Illustrate point by Greek word for "love" in text).
2. Gentle rebuke here, as if asking Judas to name his deed.
3. Meditation on the effects of evil action usually is a restraining influence.

III. REJECTION OF CHRIST'S LOVE.

1. In spite of every appeal, man has power to refuse.
2. Limit may be exceeded by those whose opportunities have been the most favorable.
3. Sin is progressive. In the life of Judas, its steps were:
   (1) Reproving Mary.
   (2) Bargaining with chief priests.
   (3) Betrayal.

Conclusion.—Stay the progress of sin by admitting into life the love of God.

From the words Jesus addressed to Judas, "Friend, wherefore art thou come?" the author here makes three inferences. In the first place, he showed the patience of Christ's love. Of all persons who had proved unfaithful to Jesus, Judas was undoubtedly the worst. If Jesus was ever justified in uttering a rebuke to any man, Judas was certainly that man. But there was no impatience, no rebuke, but only an illustration of the fact that the love of Christ can go to the limit and that it passeth all understanding.

In the next place, he draws the inference that Christ pleads with man, and that while His appeal is without limit, nevertheless our continuance in sin does modify that love. As the word "friend" fell upon the ears of Judas, a feeling of shame must have passed over him as he felt the pleading of his Master. It must have almost been as if Jesus said, "Can you do this, Judas?"

The last inference is that the rejection of Christ is possible even for one who has had a very close knowledge of Him. It thus implies the possibility of rejection even by those who are the least excusable.

Inferential sermons are the most difficult of all to prepare. The one just given illustrates some of the qualities necessary. It reveals a very skillful use of the text, a deep insight into human nature, and a fine appreciation of Christ's inner character. The development of each division leads directly to a point where a personal application is made. Only a great preacher could construct such a sermon. The chief danger of sermons of this class is to make inferences that are "far-fetched," that are really not inferences at all, but are the product of the fancy, rather than legitimate deductions from texts or his-torical situations.

While certain of these types of sermons have advantages over others, it is really desirable to use all of these methods. To follow any one of them alone would produce the effect of sameness or monotony. Whatever method of development is followed, however, the really important thing is to make one's sermons fresh and original, for when they fail in this quality they are a failure, no matter what method is used.

QUESTIONS ON CHAPTER IX.

1. Prepare a textual sermon.

2. Do you observe any dangers from the use of the textual sermon?

3. What advantages are there in the use of the topical sermon?

4. What dangers are there to the preacher in the topical sermon?

5. What is necessary in order to make an expository sermon interesting?

6. Can you give any reason why there is so little expository preaching done in modern times?

7. Why are inferential sermons difficult?

8. Can a sermon be a combination, having one division on the expository method, another based on inference, and another topical?

CHAPTER X.

COLLECTING MATERIAL

YOUNG preachers, who have not used any definite methods of collecting material, will be interested to know some of the principal methods that are used, and have some suggestions regarding the value of each.

At the outset it must be understood that all knowledge is useful to a preacher. There is nothing in the way of information under heaven that may not help him at some time or other in his work. In addition to the Bible, such subjects as history, science, psychology, philosophy, literature, sociology and political economy all have their place.

Not only knowledge gained through books, however, but also that received through experience, is valuable. Few experiences in life are without benefit to the alert mind. Visits with the sick, conversations while traveling, talks in the homes—indeed, everywhere one goes, whatever he does—furnishes him with material for thought on life's needs and problems, and especially as these relate to the spiritual world.

We wish here, however, to discuss material of a more definite and tangible nature, such as clippings from papers and magazines. Some uniform and permanent system of preserving these is a very desirable thing for every preacher to have. Not only must he save these articles, but he must have them available

131

in such a form that they can be utilized on very short notice. Statistics are specially helpful, as they give originality to discourse along the line of intensive study, and any good contributions to periodicals on such subjects as education, prohibition, patriotism or religion, are almost certain to be needed by the preacher at some time or other. In what form, then, shall the preacher save these materials?

The first method to notice is a *system of large envelopes,* indexed according to the subject. As one reads articles of value in papers or magazines, he cuts them out and places them in these envelopes. Then, when he wants material for a sermon or an address, all he has to do is to take the envelope, and the material is all there for him, and all he needs to do is to review and arrange it. This enables any one subscribing for periodicals to scan them in his spare time and cut from them the articles that appeal to him as having value for his work. So that, while he is reading the paper, he is systematically enriching his treasure for use in the time of need. As he goes through his periodicals in this way in his leisure, he is appropriating for future use the best in them, and by this process he reduces to a minimum the work required in preparing sermons and addresses.

A second method is to keep what might be termed a *scrap-book.* The purpose of this is to keep brief statements of fact, poetical quotations, extracts from correspondence that have moral and spiritual significance, and anything else that might be worth saving. A large book something like a large photograph album can be used for this purpose, and this will in the course of time become a veritable gold mine of thought. Some kind of a very general classification can also be adopted with this system.

Then, a third plan can be followed by those who subscribe for periodicals with sermonic material in them, and who desire to save the best sermons. The form in which they come makes them too bulky to place in the envelopes. To preserve these, *large folders,* made of cardboard, or even brown paper, may be used. These cuttings can then be numbered and indexed according to text and subject, and as one begins to prepare his sermon, if it be on a text, all that he has to do is to look up the index and see if he has any material along the line of development that he expects to follow. Or, if he is preaching on a subject, he can turn to his index again for help in that direction. Where there is very little in the sermon that can be appropriated directly, it will almost always be found (if the sermon was worth saving) that if on the same subject there will be suggestions and illustrations that will be helpful. This plan might seem to be a rather cumbersome one, but from experience it can be recommended as one of the most time-saving, suggestive and fruitful means of sermon preparation.

Another plan is here suggested in connection with the *reading of books.* Some write freely on the margin of books they read, so that with but little trouble they can locate any extract that they wish to use. From borrowed books, however, a few pointed sentences ought to be saved, so that in any future reference to the book it is possible to quote exactly, if necessary. If one can be definite and specific in his statements, it helps to inspire confidence, and this is the quality par excellence in the speaker. It is not a very difficult matter for one to note a few sentences or extracts from books that are being read, and when these are copied into a memorandum-book they become a permanent possession. To put it in the language of another:

"When reading authors, when you find
Bright passages that strike your mind,
Be not contented with the sight,
But take them down in black and white:
Such a respect is wisely shown
As makes another's thought one's own."

It requires very little time, it helps one to read with discrimination, and enables one to be specific in speaking.

The last method to suggest is one which has its chief value for students, and those who are continually traveling, or attending conventions. This is the *vest-pocket memorandum-book*. This is used to jot down briefly illustrations, outlines of addresses, epigrammatic sayings and observations and other points of value. This often proves a mine of thought when traveling, or when one is away from home, and so does not have other sources of material at hand. Certain it is that any one who goes through life separating the wheat from the chaff will always have something fresh and interesting to say, and will not only accumulate material, but will also develop the power of observation, and so acquire the process of spiritual selection that he will be able to conserve the best of the past for the use of the present and the good of the future.

In gathering the materials for sermons, the important thing is not the method, but that we have *some* system. After having decided to preach from some text or subject, it is very helpful indeed to be able to go to a storehouse and find exactly what is wanted in the way of material. A man may be a cashier in the bank and handle large sums of money, but remain a very poor man. A preacher may do a great deal of reading and not have any way of saving his material beyond what he can remember, and when the time of need comes he has little or nothing; while another may read less and remember little, but he finds his savings a very present help in time of need. Not what goes into the net counts, but what remains.

QUESTIONS ON CHAPTER X.

1. Which method of collecting material appeals to you most? Give the reason for your selection.